TIME
FOR KIDS

KIDS IN THE KITCHEN
Cookbook
FUN RECIPES FOR KIDS TO MAKE!

TIME FOR KIDS

Managing Editor: Nellie Gonzalez Cutler
Editor, Time Learning Ventures: Jonathan Rosenbloom

R STUDIO T

Concept and Book Packaging: R studio T, New York City
Art Directors and Designers: Raúl Rodriguez & Rebecca Tachna
Writer: Sandra Kilpatrick Jordan
Illustrator: Chris Reed
Designer: Tom Koken
Photographer: Craig Deutsch
Food Stylists: Jeff Dresser, Steve Sant
Copy Editor: Krissy Roleke
Photo Researcher: Elizabeth Vezzulla
Image Editor: John Whitley
Food Consultant: Amanda Perin

Food Editor: Katherine Cobbs

In loving memory of
Rebecca Tachna

Acknowledgments

Rachel West, Mackenzie Cogle, Chere Bell, Jenna Bell,
Amore St. Ives, Ryan Lee, Sarai Arriaga, Sara Noriega,
Gerardo Contreras, Jacques Pavlenyi, Michael Loria

Photo Credits

COVER (CLOCKWISE FROM TOP): Becky Luigart-Stayner;
Jim Bathie; American Images Inc./
Getty Images; Rob Stark/shutterstock
28, 33, 61, 75, 87, 91, 95 (TOP AND BOTTOM), 107,
113, 125, 127: John Autry; 41 (MIDDLE); 63: Iain Bagwell;
3 (BOTTOM), 14–15 (BOTTOM), 25, 35, 41 (BOTTOM RIGHT), 43, 46, 55, 65,
71, 72 (RIGHT), 74, 76, 78, 85, 88, 89, 101, 105, 111, 119, 123, 130,
131 (LEFT), 136, 137, 145, 149, 151, 153: Jim Bathie;
79: Van Chaplin; 90, 117: Jennifer Davick; 3 (TOP), 6,
10, 14–15 (LEFT, TOP, RIGHT), 17, 19, 21, 27, 31, 37, 39,
41 (TOP), 49, 57, 69, 72 (LEFT), 73, 77, 81, 83, 93, 109, 121,
131 (RIGHT), 133: Craig Deutsch; 97: Lee Harrelson;
23, 45, 51, 58, 115, 135, 139, 143: Beth Dreiling Hontzas;
94, 103, 129, 147: Becky Luigart-Stayner;
40–41 (BOTTOM), 53, 67: Randy Mayor; 141: John O'Hagan;
9: Top 5 illustration by Dave Klug for TIME FOR KIDS;
SPOT PHOTOGRAPHY (ALL SHUTTERSTOCK UNLESS INDICATED OTHERWISE):
7: kosam; fritka/iStockphoto; nito; Kitch Bain; Gavran333;
Africa Studio; Ganko; Africa Studio; M. Unal Ozmen;
Keith Bell; nito; shutswis; Boleslaw Kubica; Artistic
Endeavor; Craig Deutsch; Shawn Hempel; Stillfx;
ribeiroantonio; 17: Tamara Kulikova; 35: Sergio33;
49: Randy Mayor/Getty Images; 74: Vtls; 85: Betacam-SP;
98: Nattika; 132: AntoinetteW; 148: redefine images; 160: Ganko
BACK COVER: All by Craig Deutsch except
Puddin' Heads by Jim Bathie
PHOTO STYLISTS: Kay Clarke, Katherine Eckert Coyne,
Mary Louise Menendez

Time HOME ENTERTAINMENT

Publisher Jim Childs
Vice President, Business Development & Strategy Steven Sandonato
Executive Director, Marketing Services Carol Pittard
Executive Director, Retail & Special Sales Tom Mifsud
Executive Publishing Director Joy Butts
Director, Bookazine Development & Marketing Laura Adam
Finance Director Glenn Buonocore
Associate Publishing Director Megan Pearlman
Assistant General Counsel Helen Wan
Assistant Director, Special Sales Ilene Schreider
Senior Book Production Manager Susan Chodakiewicz
Design & Prepress Manager Anne-Michelle Gallero
Brand Manager Jonathan White
Associate Prepress Manager Alex Voznesenskiy
Associate Production Manager Kimberly Marshall
Assistant Brand Manager Stephanie Braga

Editorial Director Stephen Koepp
Editorial Operations Director Michael Q. Bullerdick

Special Thanks: Katherine Barnet, Jeremy Biloon, Rose Cirrincione,
Lauren Hall Clark, Jacqueline Fitzgerald, Christine Font, Jenna Goldberg,
Hillary Hirsch, David Kahn, Suzanne Janso, Raphael Joa, Amy Mangus,
Robert Marasco, Amy Migliaccio, Nina Mistry, Dave Rozzelle,
Ricardo Santiago, Adriana Tierno, Vanessa Wu

Contents

How to Get Cooking with This Book 4

Follow These Kitchen Basics 6

Smart Food Choices Mean Good Eats 8

How to Avoid Kitchen Disasters 10

You Can Measure 12

Metric Equivalents 13

1 Rev Up with Breakfast 14

2 Time for Lunch 40

3 Sides and Snacks 72

4 Ready for Dinner 94

5 What's for Dessert? 130

Glossary 154

Recipe Index 156

General Index 158

How Sweet It Is! (A TFK Word Search Puzzle) 160

How to Get
Cooking with This Book

The **TFK Kids in the Kitchen Cookbook** puts kids in the kitchen, creating delicious meals and snacks. Healthy recipes will fuel your body for school and after-school activities. With this book you will:

● Learn where food comes from before it reaches the grocery store.

● Become kitchen-safety smart.

As you go through the book, here's what you'll find:

Color Bar: Differently colored borders let you quickly see what chapter you're in (see chart on page 5).

Difficulty: This tells you whether the recipe will be simple, moderately easy, or difficult to prepare.

Servings: This tells you how many people the recipe will feed and it may also give the size of each portion.

Sidebars: Learn fascinating food facts, cooking trivia and history, tips for healthier eating, and essential first-timer cooking terms.

Ready for
Dinner

SIMPLE

Try This
Be environmentally friendly. Consider selecting cod that is caught by hook and line rather than by dragnets.

Feast on This
March 14 is National Potato Chip Day.

Crushed and Crusty
Chips-and-Fish

Here's a delicious update on the classic fish-and-chips recipe. The tang in the salt-and-vinegar chips mellows as the fish bake in the oven.

Makes: 4 fillets

98

- Organize your meals by making shopping lists so you don't forget anything.
- Chop, freeze, roast, toast, bake, julienne, and sauté foods.
- Impress your friends and family with delightfully delicious foods.
- Turn your parent into your kitchen assistant.
- Get to build ice-cream sandwiches and perfect parfaits!

What Color Is My Meal?

Differently colored borders let you quickly see what chapter you're in.

BREAKFAST

LUNCH

SIDES AND SNACKS

DINNER

DESSERT

Ingredients: Each item in the recipe is listed in the order it will be used. This list indicates how each item should be readied (chopped and so on) and how much you'll need.

Preparation: These steps tell you how to combine your ingredients, and in what order. Be sure to read the recipe from beginning to end before making the dish, so you'll know what to expect, including what utensils and cookware you'll need.

From TIME FOR KIDS: Little-known facts, fun stats, and mini articles from issues of TIME FOR KIDS magazine and *TFK Around the World*.

Nutritional Information: Important elements of each recipe's nutrition are itemized here, including calories, fiber, sodium, fats, and carbohydrates.

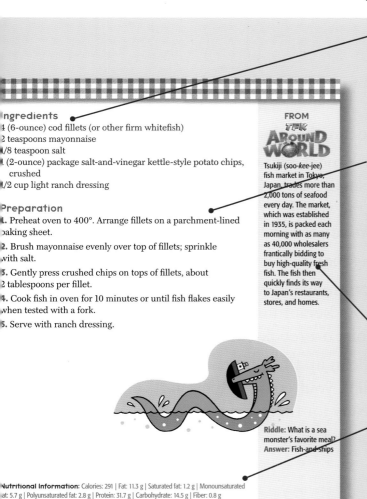

Ingredients
4 (6-ounce) cod fillets (or other firm whitefish)
2 teaspoons mayonnaise
1/8 teaspoon salt
1 (2-ounce) package salt-and-vinegar kettle-style potato chips, crushed
1/2 cup light ranch dressing

Preparation
1. Preheat oven to 400°. Arrange fillets on a parchment-lined baking sheet.
2. Brush mayonnaise evenly over top of fillets; sprinkle with salt.
3. Gently press crushed chips on tops of fillets, about 2 tablespoons per fillet.
4. Cook fish in oven for 10 minutes or until fish flakes easily when tested with a fork.
5. Serve with ranch dressing.

FROM
TFK
AROUND WORLD

Tsukiji (soo-*kee*-jee) fish market in Tokyo, Japan, trades more than 2,000 tons of seafood every day. The market, which was established in 1935, is packed each morning with as many as 40,000 wholesalers frantically bidding to buy high-quality fresh fish. The fish then quickly finds its way to Japan's restaurants, stores, and homes.

Riddle: What is a sea monster's favorite meal?
Answer: Fish-and-ships

Nutritional Information: Calories: 291 | Fat: 11.3 g | Saturated fat: 1.2 g | Monounsaturated fat: 5.7 g | Polyunsaturated fat: 2.8 g | Protein: 31.7 g | Carbohydrate: 14.5 g | Fiber: 0.8 g | Cholesterol: 79 mg | Iron: 1.4 mg | Sodium: 549 mg | Calcium: 49 mg

99

Follow These
Kitchen Basics

Here are some tips to help you get started:

- Always get the okay to cook from mom or dad. You'll need an adult on hand as your *sous-chef* (*soo*-shef)—that's French for "assistant cook."

- Choose a simple recipe and read it all the way through. Do you have every ingredient you need? If not, make a shopping list and have a grown-up take you to pick up these items at the grocery store.

- Before you begin:
  - Prep your kitchen for safety and cleanliness: Use the tips on page 10.
  - Wear an apron, tie long hair back, wash hands.
  - With an adult, wash, peel, and chop your ingredients, and set them aside in small bowls. Getting all your ingredients ready before cooking is called *mise en place* (*meez* ahn plahs), which is French for "everything in its place."
  - Set out the cooking tools you'll need.

- Carefully follow each step of the recipe from beginning to end. Set a timer so foods don't overcook or burn.

- Clean up the kitchen afterward. Make sure all of your cooking tools and counters are ready for the preparation of the next meal.

- Don't forget to have fun cooking!

The Young Chef's Toolbox

The recipes in this book suggest using the following kitchen tools. We've added a few more to help you stay safe and to keep things clean. Discuss what you need with an adult; come up with alternate tools if needed.

disinfecting hand soap

apron

hot pads

cutting boards

vegetable peeler

whisk

knives for chopping (adults)

mixing bowls

measuring cups and spoons

blender

mixer

Dutch oven or skillet

baking sheets and jelly-roll pan

colander

spatula

tongs

You will also need: Wooden spoon, waffle iron, waxed paper, parchment paper, aluminum foil, plastic wrap, kitchen timer, wire cooling racks, springform pan, serving dishes and utensils, plates, bowls, mugs, microwave-safe bowls, parfait or dessert glasses, cutlery, napkins, paper towels, storage containers with lids, zip-top plastic bags, disinfecting wipes, dish soap

Smart Food Choices Mean
Good Eats

It's easy and fun to make delicious food. Eating healthy foods provides your brain and body with the right amount of energy, just when you need it.

Natural, brightly colored foods are often the most nutritious. The colors in fresh fruits, vegetables, grains, and beans indicate high levels of antioxidants, vitamins, and disease-fighting phytochemicals. Here are some examples of the best foods for you:

- **Fruits:** Apples, bananas, berries, grapefruits, grapes, lemons, limes, oranges, pineapples
- **Vegetables:** Avocados, broccoli, carrots, green beans, onions, potatoes, spinach, squash, tomatoes, zucchinis
- **Grains** such as corn, rice, wheat; **nuts and seeds** such as almonds, peanuts, sunflower seeds, walnuts; **legumes** such as beans, lentils, peas
- **Protein:** Beef, chicken, lamb, fish, shellfish, soy-based foods such as tofu
- **Dairy:** Milk, butter, cheese, buttermilk, yogurt

Power Foods

Power foods give you the richest amount of nutrients, the least amount of calories, and the most health benefits. Below are some we love. Remember, even foods that are good for you should be eaten in moderation.

- Avocados, beans, dark berries, dark chocolate, mushrooms, oatmeal, olive oil, peanut butter, pomegranates, pumpkins, salmon, spinach, turkey and other lean meats, whole grains

Try This

When shopping for groceries, visit the produce section first. Look for colorful fruits and vegetables. Try choosing one or two fruits and vegetables in each color. For a real adventure, try an unfamiliar fruit or vegetable each week.

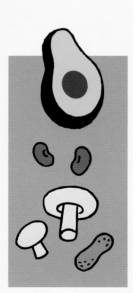

Stay-Fit Tips

- Fill half your plate with fruits and vegetables at every meal.
- Avoid eating too many foods that are packaged or processed, such as canned spaghetti, sugared cereals, powdered dip and soup mixes, boxed stovetop dinners, and artificial fruit drinks.
- Switch to fat-free or low-fat milk.
- Drink water instead of sugary drinks.
- Cut back on salt.
- Get one hour of exercise every day and work up a sweat.
- If you're between 5 and 12 years old, get 10 to 11 hours of sleep each night.

TOP 5 Goals for Good Health

TFK asked kids what health goals they'd like an adult's help to achieve. The bar graph shows what they said.

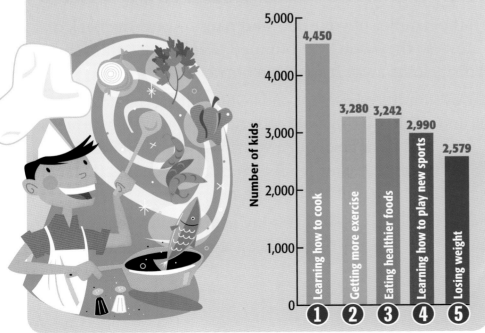

Number of kids

Goal	Number of kids
① Learning how to cook	4,450
② Getting more exercise	3,280
③ Eating healthier foods	3,242
④ Learning how to play new sports	2,990
⑤ Losing weight	2,579

Sources: Kidshealth.org and TIME For Kids

The U.S. government has issued guidelines that show the food types—and amounts—meals should include.

Fruits · Grains · Dairy · Vegetables · Protein

Choose**MyPlate**.gov

How to Avoid
Kitchen Disasters

As much fun as cooking can be, dangers may lurk in the kitchen. Everyone in your family can practice these important tips for keeping things safe and clean.

Keeping It Real Safe

- Ask an adult to chop, slice, peel, and grate your recipe's ingredients. Always be careful around knives and sharp edges: Even a potato peeler can cut your skin.

- Keep the kitchen floor clear. Clean up spills right away so that no one slips. It's a good idea to keep pets and little children out of the kitchen while you cook.

- Don't text, surf the Web, play games, or talk on the phone while cooking—these distractions could lead to an accident.

- Turn the handles of your pots and pans toward the back of the stove so they won't get bumped. Keep long hair, sleeves, and dish cloths away from stove burners.

- Wear oven mitts or use hot pads when lifting the lids off of pans and while stirring hot foods on the stove. Hot surfaces and steam can burn your skin in an instant, so protect your hands, arms, and face. Again, have an adult help out or supervise.

- Stay nearby and keep your eye on the food while it's

cooking. Set a timer so that food does not overcook, and check occasionally to make sure the heat is not turned up too high.

- Keep a fire extinguisher handy, away from the stove.

- Post a list of emergency telephone numbers near the stove, where the whole family can see it. If someone gets burned or cut, or if a fire starts, don't be afraid to call!

Keeping It Real Clean

- Wash your hands with disinfectant soap before and after you cook, and also after you handle raw meat or fish.

- If raw fish or meat touches the countertop or cutting board, wash the surfaces with hot water and soap right away.

- Before and after cooking, wipe down sink faucets, refrigerator handles, stove, cupboards, and trash cans. Use disinfecting spray or wipes—these will kill germs on contact.

- Let dishcloths dry out between uses; most bacteria thrive only in moistness. Rags should be washed in the washing machine and dried on high heat.

- Use separate sponges for washing dishes and cleaning counters. Try wetting your sponges and microwaving them for two minutes—this eliminates germs.

You Can
Measure

If the ingredient is ...

● **DRY** like flour, sugar, or salt: Scoop it with a measuring spoon or into a metal or plastic cup until you have more than you need. Brown sugar should be firmly packed down. Level it off with the back of a table knife until it is even with the rim.

● **WET** like milk, melted butter, or water: Pour into the measuring spoon or a clear glass measuring cup until it is at the rim, or at the correct line of measure. Bend down to check it at eye level for accuracy.

● **WET and THICK** like tomato paste, mustard, or ice cream: Scoop more than you need into the spoon or cup. Press it down with a spoon or spatula to fill completely, then level it with the back of a table knife.

Metric Equivalents

The recipes that appear in this cookbook use the standard U.S. method for measuring liquid and dry or solid ingredients (teaspoons, tablespoons, and cups). The information in the following charts is provided to help cooks outside the United States successfully use these recipes. All equivalents are approximate.

Common Types of Ingredients

A standard cup measure of a dry or solid ingredient will vary in weight depending on the type of ingredient. A standard cup of liquid is the same volume for any type of liquid. Use the following chart when converting standard cup measures to grams (weight) or milliliters (volume).

Standard Cup	Fine Powder (e.g., flour)	Grain (e.g., rice)	Granular (e.g., sugar)	Liquid Solids (e.g., butter)	Liquid (e.g., milk)
1	140 g	150 g	190 g	200 g	240 ml
$3/4$	105 g	113 g	143 g	150 g	180 ml
$2/3$	93 g	100 g	125 g	133 g	160 ml
$1/2$	70 g	75 g	95 g	100 g	120 ml
$1/3$	47 g	50 g	63 g	67 g	80 ml
$1/4$	35 g	38 g	48 g	50 g	60 ml
$1/8$	18 g	19 g	24 g	25 g	30 ml

Liquid Ingredients by Volume

$1/4$ tsp		=		1 ml
$1/2$ tsp		=		2 ml
1 tsp		=		5 ml
3 tsp	= 1 Tbsp	= $1/2$ fl oz	=	15 ml
	2 Tbsp	= $1/8$ cup = 1 fl oz	=	30 ml
	4 Tbsp	= $1/4$ cup = 2 fl oz	=	60 ml
	$5 1/3$ Tbsp	= $1/3$ cup = 3 fl oz	=	80 ml
	8 Tbsp	= $1/2$ cup = 4 fl oz	=	120 ml
	$10 2/3$ Tbsp	= $2/3$ cup = 5 fl oz	=	160 ml
	12 Tbsp	= $3/4$ cup = 6 fl oz	=	180 ml
	16 Tbsp	= 1 cup = 8 fl oz	=	240 ml
	1 pt	= 2 cups = 16 fl oz	=	480 ml
	1 qt	= 4 cups = 32 fl oz	=	960 ml
		33 fl oz	=	1,000 ml = 1 l

Dry Ingredients by Weight

(To convert ounces to grams, multiply the number of ounces by 30.)

1 oz	=	$1/16$ lb	=	30 g
4 oz	=	$1/4$ lb	=	120 g
8 oz	=	$1/2$ lb	=	240 g
12 oz	=	$3/4$ lb	=	360 g
16 oz	=	1 lb	=	480 g

Length

(To convert inches to centimeters, multiply the number of inches by 2.5.)

1 in		=		2.5 cm
6 in	= $1/2$ ft	=		15 cm
12 in	= 1 ft	=		30 cm
36 in	= 3 ft	= 1 yd	=	90 cm
40 in		=	100 cm	= 1 m

Cooking/Oven Temperatures

	Fahrenheit	Celsius	Gas Mark
Freeze water	32°F	0°C	
Room temperature	68°F	20°C	
Boil water	212°F	100°C	
Bake	325°F	160°C	3
	350°F	180°C	4
	375°F	190°C	5
	400°F	200°C	6
	425°F	220°C	7
Broil/Grill	450°F	230°C	8

g = gram; ml = milliliter; tsp = teaspoon; Tbsp = tablespoon; fl oz = fluid ounce; pt = pint; qt = quart; l = liter; oz = ounce; lb = pound; in = inches; cm = centimeter; ft = feet; yd = yard; m = meter

CHAPTER 1

Rev Up with Breakfast

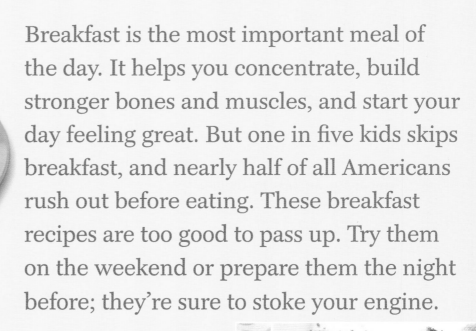

Breakfast is the most important meal of the day. It helps you concentrate, build stronger bones and muscles, and start your day feeling great. But one in five kids skips breakfast, and nearly half of all Americans rush out before eating. These breakfast recipes are too good to pass up. Try them on the weekend or prepare them the night before; they're sure to stoke your engine.

- Blueberry and Maple-Pecan Granola Parfaits
- Lemon Tart Poppy Seed Muffins
- Bacon and Egg Breakfast Pizzas
- Sausage and Egg Dusty-Trail Burritos

And many more yummy treats!

Maple-Pecan
Granola Crunch

Granola is a uniquely American breakfast cereal. Here's how to make your own. And you can store it in an airtight container for up to one week—if it lasts that long!

Makes: 16 servings (serving size: 1/4 cup)

Ingredients

Cooking spray
2 cups regular oats
1/2 cup pecan pieces
1/2 cup maple syrup
1/4 cup packed brown sugar
2 tablespoons canola oil
1/8 teaspoon salt

Preparation

1. Preheat oven to 300°. Coat a large jelly-roll pan with cooking spray.

2. Combine oats, pecan pieces, syrup, brown sugar, oil, and salt. Spread mixture evenly in pan.

3. Bake in oven for 40 to 45 minutes, stirring every 15 minutes. Cool completely.

Know Your Ingredients

Granola was invented more than 150 years ago. Instead of oats for healthy fiber, it was made using crumbled sheets of "graham" flour. Sylvester Graham invented the flour and the yummy Graham cracker.

preheat to heat the oven, pan, or pot before cooking begins

Nutritional Information: Calories: 129 | Fat: 5.2 g | Saturated fat: 0.6 g
Monounsaturated fat: 2.7 g | Polyunsaturated fat: 1.7 g | Protein: 2.2 g
Carbohydrate: 19.3 g | Fiber: 1.9 g | Cholesterol: 0 mg | Iron: 0.8 mg | Sodium: 21 mg
Calcium: 20 mg

Blueberry and Maple-Pecan
Granola Parfaits

Breakfast cereal hits the healthy sweet spot when you add colorful blueberries to the bowl. Layer them with your latest batch of homemade Maple-Pecan Granola Crunch (see page 16) for a perfect parfait.

Makes: **4 parfaits**

Ingredients

2 cups vanilla
    fat-free yogurt
2 cups blueberries
1 cup Maple-Pecan
    Granola Crunch

Preparation

1. Divide the ingredients evenly among 4 dessert glasses. For each glass, layer 1/4 cup yogurt, then 1/4 cup blueberries, and 1/4 cup Maple-Pecan granola.

2. Add another 1/4 cup yogurt and top with 1/4 cup blueberries.

SIMPLE

Feast on This

Parfait (par-*fay*) means "perfect" in French. Parfaits in the U.S. are made of layers of creamy, sweet, and crunchy foods served in tall, narrow glasses. As for ingredients, almost anything goes!

Try This

When selecting your blueberries, look for those that are firm, plump, and fully colored. Stay away from soft berries. Store them at room temperature or refrigerate in a single layer. Use within a day or two. Wash when ready to use.

Nutritional Information: Calories: 283 | Fat: 5.6 g | Saturated fat: 0.8 g
Monounsaturated fat: 2.8 g | Polyunsaturated fat: 1.8 g | Protein: 8.8 g | Carbohydrate: 50.9 g
Fiber: 3.7 g | Cholesterol: 2 mg | Iron: 1.1 mg | Sodium: 106 mg | Calcium: 242 mg

Apricot-Almond
Bits 'n' Pieces Granola

Here's another type of granola that you can eat for a grab-and-go breakfast or as a snack. Crunchy nuts, chewy fruits, and honey make this a winner!

Try This

To save time, buy dried fruits and nuts that are already chopped.

Fluids clear your throat. Honey soothes it. Adding two teaspoons of honey to tea or lemon water can help you reduce coughing.

Makes: 6 cups (serving size: 1/3 cup)

Ingredients

2-3/4 cups regular oats
1/2 cup slivered almonds
1/2 cup dried cherries
1/2 cup coarsely chopped dried apricots
1/3 cup coarsely chopped walnuts
1/3 cup golden raisins
1/2 cup honey
1/3 cup butter, melted

Preparation

1. Preheat oven to 350°.

2. Combine oats, almonds, cherries, apricots, walnuts, and raisins in a medium bowl.

3. In a separate bowl, stir honey and butter together until well mixed.

4. Drizzle the honey mixture over the oat mixture; stir until well coated.

5. Spread mixture in a single layer in a jelly-roll pan. Bake for 15 minutes, then stir. Bake an additional 10 minutes or until lightly browned.

6. Cool completely in the pan. Break into pieces to serve or store in an airtight container up to a week.

Nutritional Information: Calories: 164 | Fat: 6 g | Saturated fat: 2 g | Monounsaturated fat: 2 g | Polyunsaturated fat: 1.6 g | Protein: 3.3 g | Carbohydrate: 25.4 g | Fiber: 2.6 g Cholesterol: 7 mg | Iron: 1 mg | Sodium: 20 mg | Calcium: 25 mg

Feast on This

Cave paintings show that the practice of honey collection and beekeeping dates back to the Stone Age.

Cereals with the Most Sugar

Many cereals may seem "magically delicious" because they contain an unhealthy amount of sugar (Honey Smacks are 56% sugar by weight). Here are the cereals with the most sugar:

1. Kellogg's Honey Smacks
2. Post Golden Crisp
3. Kellogg's Froot Loops Marshmallow
4. Quaker Oats Cap'n Crunch's Oops! All Berries
5. Quaker Oats Original Cap'n Crunch

Source: Environmental Working Group

Lemon Tart
Poppy Seed Muffins

Feast on This

"Have You Seen The Muffin Man?" is a traditional English children's song. In Victorian times, muffins and other foods were often delivered door-to-door, so it makes sense that everyone would be looking for him.

Poppy-Seed-Producing Countries

Each year, a total of more than 102,600 tons of poppy seeds are produced by these countries:

1. Turkey
2. Czech Republic
3. Spain
4. France
5. Croatia

Source: Food and Agriculture Organization of the United Nations, Agricultural Production data, 2010

Make these muffins after school and eat them for breakfast the next morning.

Makes: **12 muffins**

Ingredients

1-3/4 cups all-purpose flour
3/4 cup sugar
2-1/2 teaspoons baking powder
1/2 teaspoon baking soda
1/2 teaspoon salt
1 tablespoon grated lemon rind
  (about 1 medium-size lemon)
1 tablespoon poppy seeds
1-1/4 cups low-fat buttermilk
2 tablespoons butter, melted
1 large egg, lightly beaten

Preparation

1. Preheat oven to 400°. Place a muffin liner in each cup of a 12-cup muffin tin.

2. Add flour to large mixing bowl.

3. Add sugar, baking powder, baking soda, and salt; stir well with a whisk.

4. Measure and stir in lemon rind and poppy seeds. Make a well in center of mixture.

5. In a separate bowl, combine buttermilk, butter, and egg; stir with a whisk to combine. Add to well in flour mixture, stirring just until moist.

6. Spoon batter into muffin cups, filling 3/4 full. Bake for 20 to 22 minutes or until golden brown.

7. Cool in pan for 5 minutes on a wire rack, then remove from pan. Place muffins directly on wire rack to cool completely.

Nutritional Information: Calories: 154 | Fat: 3 g | Saturated fat: 1.5 g | Monounsaturated fat: 0.78 g | Polyunsaturated fat: 0.41 g | Protein: 3.5 g | Carbohydrate: 28 g | Fiber: 0.6 g Cholesterol: 24 mg | Iron: 1 mg | Sodium: 282 mg | Calcium: 93 mg

Know Your Ingredients

The yellow skin of a lemon, called the rind, contains oils that give foods a fresh flavor. With an adult's help, use a cheese grater to remove the lemon rind. Avoid the bitter white layer just below.

FROM
TIME
FOR KIDS

In 2012, at just 12 years old, Lizzie Marie Likness was already a successful chef. Her love of cooking began at the age of 2, when she'd help her mom make applesauce. Five years later, she had her own company and online cooking show featuring healthy recipes. Go, Lizzie!

Cinnamon Streusel
Applesauce Muffins

These yummy muffins are a fun wake-and-take breakfast for your family. Make them the night before and store in an airtight container.

Makes: 12 muffins and 1 cup streusel topping

Ingredients

Cinnamon Streusel Topping
1/3 cup granulated sugar
1/4 cup firmly packed light brown sugar
3 tablespoons all-purpose baking mix (such as Bisquick)
1/4 teaspoon ground cinnamon
2 tablespoons butter, melted

Applesauce Muffins
Cooking spray
4 cups all-purpose baking mix
1/2 cup sugar
2 teaspoons ground cinnamon
2/3 cup chunky applesauce
1/2 cup milk
1/4 cup vegetable oil
2 large eggs

Preparation
Part One: Cinnamon Streusel Topping

1. Whisk together sugar, brown sugar, baking mix, and cinnamon in a medium bowl until blended.

2. Stir butter into sugar mixture until well blended and crumbly.

Know Your Ingredients

Applesauce first appeared in 18th-century British cookbooks, and to this day, Europeans still prefer it mixed with meats. In the United States, applesauce is a favorite side dish or dessert.

Part Two: Applesauce Muffins

1. Preheat oven to 400°. Lightly grease a 12-cup muffin pan with vegetable oil or cooking spray.

2. Whisk together baking mix, sugar, and cinnamon in a large bowl; make a well in center of mixture.

3. In a separate bowl, whisk together applesauce, milk, oil, and eggs. Add to sugar mixture, stirring until dry ingredients are moistened.

4. Spoon batter into muffin pan, filling cups almost completely full.

5. Sprinkle Cinnamon Streusel Topping over batter.

6. Bake for 18 to 20 minutes or until a wooden toothpick inserted in the center of a muffin comes out clean and tops are golden brown. Cool 5 minutes in pan on a wire rack. Remove from pan to the wire rack; cool completely.

Nutritional Information: Calories: 323 | Fat: 14 g | Saturated fat: 4 g | Monounsaturated fat: 2.3 g | Polyunsaturated fat: 5.4 g | Protein: 5 g | Carbohydrate: 48.5 g | Fiber: 0.5 g Cholesterol: 41 mg | Iron: 1.4 mg | Sodium: 549 mg | Calcium: 68 mg

Cinnamon Growers

Cinnamon is the peeled, dried bark of a tree. Here are the spice's top growers:

1. Indonesia
2. China
3. Sri Lanka
4. Vietnam
5. Madagascar

Source: *TIME For Kids Around the World: Indonesia*

Bacon and Egg
Breakfast Pizzas

MODERATE

Bacon, cheese, and potatoes make for tasty toppings on this kid-approved morning pizza.

Makes: **8 servings (serving size: 1 wedge)**

Ingredients

Cooking spray
1 (8-ounce) can refrigerated crescent-roll dough
1 cup frozen shredded or diced hash brown
   potatoes, thawed
6 center-cut bacon slices, cooked and crumbled
1 cup (4 ounces) shredded extra-sharp cheddar cheese
8 large egg whites, lightly beaten
1/4 teaspoon salt
1/8 teaspoon freshly ground black pepper
2 tablespoons grated fresh Parmesan cheese

Preparation

1. Preheat oven to 375°. Coat a 12-inch pizza pan with cooking spray.

2. Unroll dough, and separate into triangles, according to package directions. Press triangles together to form a single 10-inch round crust on a pizza pan. Crimp outer edges of dough with fingers to form a rim.

3. Top prepared dough with potatoes, bacon, and cheddar cheese. Carefully pour egg whites over cheese; sprinkle with salt, pepper, and Parmesan cheese.

4. Bake for 23 minutes or until crust is browned. Cut into wedges.

Try This
To microwave bacon, place six slices between paper towels on a microwave-safe plate. Cook four to five minutes on high, checking every one or two minutes.

Reheat leftovers on a griddle or in a skillet over medium heat to get a crisp crust without overcooking the filling.

Nutritional Information: Calories: 192 | Fat: 10.1 g | Saturated fat: 4.9 g
Monounsaturated fat: 1.9 g | Polyunsaturated fat: 1 g | Protein: 11.6g | Carbohydrate: 14.5 g
Fiber: 0.1 g | Cholesterol: 15 mg | Iron: 1.4 mg | Sodium: 560 mg | Calcium: 132 mg

Feast on This

Humans have enjoyed eggs for thousands of years. Records from China and Egypt show that eggs were eaten as part of a meal as far back as 1400 B.C.

Sausage and Egg
Dusty-Trail Burritos

MODERATE

Make it a Tex-Mex start to your day! Roll your breakfast in a tortilla and add toppings.

Makes: **2 burritos**

Ingredients

Cooking spray
1/2 cup chopped red bell pepper
1/4 cup chopped onion
3 ounces turkey breakfast sausage
1/2 cup egg substitute
1/4 cup (1 ounce) shredded reduced-fat cheddar cheese
6 tablespoons bottled salsa, divided
2 (8-inch) fat-free flour tortillas
1/4 cup reduced-fat sour cream

Try This
You could also use two large eggs, beaten, in place of the egg substitute.

Preparation

1. Coat a nonstick skillet with cooking spray.

2. Heat skillet over medium-high heat. Add red pepper, onion, and sausage. Cook 4 minutes or until browned, stirring to crumble sausage.

3. Add egg substitute. Cook 2 minutes, stirring frequently.

4. Remove from heat. Stir in cheddar cheese and 2 tablespoons salsa. Cover mixture and let stand 2 minutes.

5. Heat tortillas according to package directions. Spoon half of the egg mixture down the center of each tortilla; roll up. Serve with remaining salsa and sour cream as toppings.

Feast on This

Long ago, Aztecs filled corn and flour flatbreads and sold them at markets. The Spanish named the flatbreads "tortillas." Legend says that cowboys in the southwestern U.S. bought stuffed tortillas for lunch from vendors who traveled on donkeys. This is how the word burrito, meaning "little donkey," was born.

Nutritional Information: Calories: 314 | Fat: 9.6 g | Saturated fat: 4.4 g
Monounsaturated fat: 3.1 g | Polyunsaturated fat: 1.8 g | Protein: 20.7 g | Carbohydrate: 26.9 g
Fiber: 3.9 g | Cholesterol: 50 mg | Iron: 2.6 mg | Sodium: 915 mg | Calcium: 148 mg

DIFFICULT

Ham and Swiss
Breakfast Grillers

Here's a hearty portable breakfast sandwich for when you're really hungry.

Makes: **4 sandwiches**

Ingredients

Cooking spray
4 ounces thinly sliced low-sodium deli ham
4 large eggs
4 English muffins, split and toasted
4 (1-ounce) slices Swiss cheese

Preparation

1. Coat a nonstick skillet with cooking spray. Preheat broiler to high.

2. Heat skillet over medium-high heat. Add ham to pan; sauté 2 minutes or until lightly browned. Remove ham from pan and set aside.

3. Recoat pan with cooking spray; return it to stove. Crack eggs into pan. Cover and cook for 4 minutes or until eggs are cooked through. Remove from heat.

4. Place 4 toasted muffin halves, cut sides up, on a baking sheet.

5. Top each half with 1 cheese slice. Broil for 2 minutes or until cheese melts.

6. Divide ham evenly between cheese-topped muffin halves. Top with 1 egg and 1 muffin half to complete your breakfast sandwich.

Nutritional Information: Calories: 344 | Fat: 14.7 g | Saturated fat: 6.7 g
Monounsaturated fat: 4.1 g | Polyunsaturated fat: 1.5 g | Protein: 23.5 g | Carbohydrate: 29.1 g
Fiber: 0 g | Cholesterol: 250 mg | Iron: 2 mg | Sodium: 553 mg | Calcium: 351 mg

Know Your Ingredients

Hard "Swiss" cheese became a staple food for 15th-century travelers in Switzerland. Mountain passes were often snowed in, so monks kept lots on hand for guests.

broiler an area of the oven that provides the highest heat and cooks food very quickly

Feast on This

The original English muffins were very different from the ones we know today. In the 1800s, they were made by mixing mashed potatoes with leftover scraps of bread dough. Then the dough was fried on a hot griddle.

Chocolate Chip
WOW! Waffles

DIFFICULT

For an awesome breakfast, serve chocolate chip waffles. They're even better topped with vanilla ice cream and chocolate mini chips for dessert.

Makes: **6 waffles**

Ingredients

Cooking spray
1-3/4 cups all-purpose flour
2 teaspoons baking powder
1/2 teaspoon salt
1-1/2 cups fat-free milk
1 tablespoon butter, melted
1 teaspoon vanilla extract
1 large egg yolk
1 large egg white
1 tablespoon sugar
1/2 cup semisweet chocolate mini chips

Preparation

1. Coat a waffle iron with cooking spray, and preheat.

2. Place flour in a large bowl; stir in baking powder and salt.

3. In another bowl, whisk together milk, butter, vanilla, and egg yolk. Add this to flour mixture, stirring until blended.

4. Beat egg white and sugar with a mixer at high speed until stiff peaks form. Fold into flour mixture. Fold in mini chips.

5. Spoon about 1/2 cup batter onto hot waffle iron, allowing batter to spread to the edges. Cook 3 to 5 minutes or until done; repeat procedure with remaining batter.

Try This
To separate egg whites, crack the egg on the edge of a bowl. Turning the egg upright, open the shell into two halves, keeping the yolk in the lower half. Pour the yolk from one shell to the other, letting only the egg white fall into the bowl.

Feast on This

In 17th-century New York City (then called New Amsterdam), Dutch settlers made quick breads called *wafels.* Eggs and yeast helped the bread dough rise before it was poured onto a hot waffle iron.

Chocolate-Loving Countries

On average, Americans spent $58 per person on chocolate in 2011. Here are the countries that spent the most per person on the sweet treat:

1. Norway
2. Ireland
3. Switzerland
4. United Kingdom
5. Austria

Source: Euromonitor International

Nutritional Information: Calories: 274 | Fat: 7.4 g | Saturated fat: 4.1 g
Monounsaturated fat: 2.4 g | Polyunsaturated fat: 0.5 g | Protein: 7.5 g
Carbohydrate: 45.4 g | Fiber: 1.8 g | Cholesterol: 42 mg | Iron: 2.4 mg | Sodium: 422 mg
Calcium: 181 mg

Banana-Chocolate
Fab French Toast

Serve this dish with a cup of mixed fruit to round out the meal. Your family will go bananas for this breakfast!

Makes: 4 servings (serving size: 3 triangles)

Ingredients

1 cup thinly sliced banana
2 teaspoons canola oil
2 large eggs, lightly beaten
1/4 cup 1% low-fat milk
3/4 teaspoon vanilla extract
1/2 teaspoon sugar
1/8 teaspoon salt
6 slices whole-grain bread
4-1/2 tablespoons hazelnut-chocolate spread
   (such as Nutella)
1-1/2 teaspoons powdered sugar

Preparation

1. Slice banana. Heat oil in a large nonstick skillet over medium-high heat.

2. Mix eggs, milk, vanilla, sugar, and salt in a shallow bowl.

3. Spread each of 3 bread slices with 1-1/2 tablespoons hazelnut-chocolate spread. Arrange 1/3 cup banana slices over each bread slice. Top sandwiches with remaining 3 bread slices.

4. Working with 1 sandwich at a time, place into milk mixture, turning gently to coat both sides.

Try This
Include a handful of hazelnuts in your daily diet. Hazelnuts have a high amount of vitamin E. Vitamin E is important in maintaining healthy skin, hair, and nails.

5. Carefully place coated sandwiches into pan. Cook 2 minutes on each side or until lightly browned. Remove from pan and let cool slightly.

6. Cut each sandwich into 4 triangles. Sprinkle evenly with powdered sugar.

Feast on This

Folklore traces the history of French toast to medieval Europe, when wealthy people and knights were expected to serve dessert. But not all knights were rich. One cheap way to impress their guests was to serve milk-soaked, toasted bread with sweet toppings.

Nutritional Information: Calories: 390 | Fat: 13.8 g | Saturated fat: 3.6 g
Monounsaturated fat: 6.8 g | Polyunsaturated fat: 3.2 g | Protein: 11.7 g
Carbohydrate: 53.6 g | Fiber: 6 g | Cholesterol: 91 mg | Iron: 2.6 mg | Sodium: 391 mg
Calcium: 115 mg

Mixed Fruit
Sunshine Smoothie

This breakfast drink is refreshingly sweet.

Makes: **4 servings (serving size: about 1 cup)**

Ingredients

1-1/2 cups peeled, chopped apricots (about 4 small apricots)
2/3 cup peeled, chopped nectarine (about 1 medium nectarine)
1 cup chopped cantaloupe
1/4 cup mango nectar (such as bottled Looza)
1/8 teaspoon grated lemon rind
1 (6-ounce) carton lemon low-fat yogurt
1/2 cup frozen mango chunks
1 cup ice cubes

Preparation

1. Combine apricots, nectarine, cantaloupe, mango nectar, lemon rind, and yogurt in a blender and blend well.

2. Add frozen mango and ice. Blend until smooth.

Try This
You can keep dried apricots, pineapples, or mangoes in your backpack for a ready-to-eat snack.

Freeze Sunshine Smoothies in ice-pop molds for a nutritious frozen treat. Just one serving provides about one-third of your vitamin C and vitamin A needs for the day.

Nutritional Information: Calories: 104 | Fat: 0.9g | Saturated fat: 0.4 g
Monounsaturated fat: 0.3 g | Polyunsaturated fat: 0.1 g | Protein: 3.4 g | Carbohydrate: 22.5 g
Fiber: 3 g | Cholesterol: 2 mg | Iron: 0.4 mg | Sodium: 36 mg | Calcium: 86 mg

Apricots originated in China and have been around for more than 4,000 years. Spanish explorers to what is now California planted this fruit in the gardens of their missions. By 1792, the first major production of apricots began, and now California produces 95% of the apricots grown in the United States.

Classic
Banana Bread

Have this for breakfast, a snack, or a dessert.

Know Your Ingredients

Not all bananas taste alike. Green bananas are hard and bitter, while fully ripened yellow bananas are soft, sweet, and creamy. Bananas flecked with just a few brown spots will be at their peak flavor, but could turn mushy. Buy bananas with unspotted yellow skins and green tips.

batter a thin mixture of flour, egg, and milk or water; it may include other ingredients

Makes: 16 servings (serving size: 1 slice, 1/2 inch wide)

Ingredients

Cooking spray
1 cup whole wheat flour
1/2 cup all-purpose flour
1 teaspoon baking powder
1 teaspoon baking soda
1/8 teaspoon salt
1/4 cup sugar
2 tablespoons butter, melted
4 medium-size very ripe bananas, peeled and mashed
1 large egg, lightly beaten

Preparation

1. Preheat oven to 350°. Coat an 8-by-4-inch loaf pan with cooking spray.

2. Combine flours, baking powder, baking soda, and salt in a large bowl.

3. In a separate bowl, combine sugar, butter, bananas, and egg. Add this to the flour mixture, stirring until it becomes a moist batter.

4. Pour batter into pan. Bake 50 to 55 minutes or until a wooden toothpick inserted in the center of the bread comes out clean.

5. Cool the bread in the pan on a wire rack for 10 minutes. Remove bread from the pan, and let it cool completely on the wire rack.

Feast on This

Baking soda and baking powder both cause baked goods to rise. When these are mixed into batter before cooking, a chemical reaction produces carbon dioxide bubbles. The heat from the oven makes these bubbles expand, causing the bread to rise. The reaction begins right away, so don't delay getting the bread into the oven, or it might fall flat!

Banana-Exporting Countries

Americans go bananas for bananas. On average, an American eats 27 pounds in a year. Ecuador exports bananas all over the world—more than 5 million tons a year.

1. Ecuador
2. Philippines
3. Costa Rica
4. Colombia
5. Guatemala

Source: *TIME FOR KIDS Around the World: Ecuador*

Nutritional Information: Calories: 85 | Fat: 2 g | Saturated fat: 0.4 g | Monounsaturated fat: 0.83 g | Polyunsaturated fat: 0.45 g | Protein: 2 g | Carbohydrate: 15.5 g | Fiber: 1.8 g Cholesterol: 13 mg | Iron: 0.6 mg | Sodium: 140 mg | Calcium: 21 mg

MODERATE

Know Your Ingredients

When toasted, pecans are crunchy and full of flavor. Place 1/4 cup chopped pecans on a paper plate and microwave on high for two minutes. Stir the nuts, then microwave for an additional one to two minutes. Keep a careful eye on the pecans to be sure they do not burn.

Fun and Fruity
De-lish Oatmeal

Early school-day mornings deserve a hearty breakfast. Make this special oatmeal for the whole family. This dish will keep you full until lunchtime.

Makes: **3 servings (serving size: about 3/4 cup)**

Ingredients

3/4 cup water
3/4 cup apple cider
1 cup organic rolled oats
1/2 teaspoon salt
1/2 cup diced pear
1/4 cup sweetened dried cranberries
1/2 teaspoon ground cinnamon
1/4 teaspoon vanilla extract
1/4 cup chopped pecans, toasted
1/4 cup fat-free milk

Preparation

1. Combine water and apple cider; bring to a boil in a large saucepan.

2. Stir in oats and salt; reduce heat to low, and cook 3 minutes, stirring occasionally.

3. Add pear, cranberries, cinnamon, and vanilla, stirring gently to combine.

4. Cook 3 minutes or until oats are tender. Stir in pecans and milk.

TOP 5

Nutrients in Oatmeal

Essential nutrients are those that the body can't make on its own. Oatmeal provides these key nutrients:

1. Manganese
2. Selenium
3. Phosphorous
4. Fiber
5. Magnesium

Source: Whfoods.com

Nutritional Information: Calories: 256 | Fat: 8.4 g | Saturated fat: 0.9 g
Monounsaturated fat: 4.2 g | Polyunsaturated fat: 2.6 g | Protein: 6.2 g | Carbohydrate: 40.6 g
Fiber: 5 g | Cholesterol: 0 mg | Iron: 1.5 mg | Sodium: 403 mg | Calcium: 56 mg

CHAPTER 2

Time for Lunch

Lunch is more than quickly snarfing down a sandwich or salad. It's a time to unwind and have some fun. Laugh, chat, and chew with your friends or family. Relax and take a break before returning to afternoon classes or weekend sports. To save you time for lunchtime fun, you can make some of these recipes ahead.

- Soba Noodles with Sweet & Spicy Shrimp
- Cheesy Roll-Up Pigs in Blankets
- Soup-er Quick Chicken Noodle Soup
- Mangia! Margherita Panini

And many more yummy treats!

Wrapped-Tight
Turkey Bites

These wraps are big, so you can pack half for your school lunch, and refrigerate the rest for tomorrow. Feel free to omit the green onions, if desired. Serve with grapes and milk.

Makes: 2 large wraps

Ingredients

1 cup coarsely chopped deli turkey breast
1 cup mixed salad greens
1/4 cup frozen whole-kernel corn, thawed and drained
1/4 cup chopped red bell pepper
2 tablespoons thinly sliced green onions
2 tablespoons light ranch dressing
2 (8-inch) whole-wheat-flour tortillas

Preparation

1. Combine turkey, salad greens, corn, red pepper, green onions, and ranch dressing in a large bowl, tossing well to coat.

2. Warm tortillas according to package directions. Divide turkey mixture evenly between each wrap. Roll up, and cut in half diagonally.

Know Your Ingredients

In 1954, Gayle and Steve Henson opened a dude ranch in California. Visitors came for the horseback riding and their homemade salad dressing, made with buttermilk, mayonnaise, herbs, and spices. Now Hidden Valley Ranch dressing is known around the world.

Feast on This

It took 20 chefs, 30 restaurant employees, 15 pounds of bacon, and 175 wraps to set the world record for the largest sandwich wrap. The winning entry was 102 feet long and held together with 1,200 toothpicks. The event brought out a crowd for a cause: raising money to build affordable housing for families in need.

Grape-Growing Countries

Italy produces more grapes than any other country. Most of the grapes are used to make wine. These are the world's biggest grape growers:

1. Italy
2. France
3. China
4. United States
5. Spain

Source: *TIME FOR KIDS Around the World: Italy*

Nutritional Information: Calories: 201 | Fat: 8.3 g | Saturated fat: 0.3 g
Monounsaturated fat: 0 g | Polyunsaturated fat: 0.1 g | Protein: 17.5 g | Carbohydrate: 14.8 g
Fiber: 4.3 g | Cholesterol: 25 mg | Iron: 1.6 mg | Sodium: 763 mg | Calcium: 81 mg

Peanut Butter & Jelly
Bagel Grillers

Most kids love lunch as much as peanut butter loves jelly. PB&J is tasty any way you make it. Here, we spread it on a mini bagel and grill it.

Makes: 6 sandwiches

Ingredients

6 mini bagels, split
6 tablespoons creamy peanut butter
6 teaspoons strawberry or grape jelly
1 tablespoon butter, melted

Preparation

1. Spread peanut butter evenly among 6 bagel halves. Spread jelly on the other 6 halves.

2. Place peanut butter halves on top of jelly halves. For best grilling results, the half with jelly should be on the bottom.

3. Brush outer sides of each bagel lightly with melted butter.

4. Cook in a preheated panini press 2 minutes or until lightly browned and grill marks appear. Serve immediately.

Be Safe
Have an adult preheat the panini press for you.

Try This
No panini press? Cook sandwiches in a grill pan on the stove.

For variety, use a toaster waffle or a warm tortilla, rather than bread. Replace jelly with honey, mayonnaise, bananas, or raisins.

Feast on This

According to folklore, an Austrian baker made the first bagel in 1683 in honor of the king of Poland. Some historians say the first written account of bagels goes back to 1610, when a law in the city of Krakow, Poland, said bagels should be given to women after they've had a baby.

Nutritional Information: Calories: 195 | Fat: 10 g | Saturated fat: 3 g
Monounsaturated fat: 4.4 g | Polyunsaturated fat: 2.5 g | Protein: 7 g | Carbohydrate: 21 g
Fiber: 1.5 g | Cholesterol: 5 mg | Iron: 2 mg | Sodium: 205 mg | Calcium: 24 mg

Pesto Presto!
Pasta Salad

Pesto, an Italian sauce made mainly from basil, is delicious on pasta. You can use whole-grain rotini or macaroni instead of tortellini. It also tastes great at room temperature.

Makes: 4 servings (serving size: about 1 cup)

Ingredients

1 (9-ounce) package fresh three-cheese tortellini
Cooking spray
1 teaspoon minced garlic
2 small zucchinis, halved lengthwise and thinly sliced
    (about 2 cups)
1 cup chopped plum tomato
1-1/2 tablespoons pesto sauce (see page 47)
1/8 teaspoon salt
2 tablespoons shredded fresh Parmesan cheese

Preparation

1. Cook pasta according to package directions, omitting salt and fat. Drain pasta in a colander over a bowl. Scoop out and save 2 tablespoons of the cooking liquid.

Try This
You can buy jars of pesto sauce and chopped garlic at the supermarket.

46

2. While pasta cooks, heat a large nonstick skillet over medium-high heat. Heavily coat pan with cooking spray. Add garlic and zucchini; sauté 5 minutes or until zucchini is tender. Remove pan from heat; add pasta and tomato to zucchini mixture, tossing gently.

3. Combine reserved 2 tablespoons cooking liquid with pesto and salt in a small bowl. Drizzle over pasta mixture, tossing gently to coat. Sprinkle with cheese.

Nutritional Information: Calories: 251 | Fat: 7.5 g | Saturated fat: 3 g | Monounsaturated fat: 2.4 g | Polyunsaturated fat: 0.69 g | Protein: 12 g | Carbohydrate: 35 g | Fiber: 3 g Cholesterol: 27 mg | Iron: 1.6 mg | Sodium: 464 mg | Calcium: 171 mg

Pesto Sauce
Ingredients
2 tablespoons coarsely chopped
   walnuts or pine nuts
2 garlic cloves, peeled
3 tablespoons extra-virgin olive oil
4 cups (about 4 ounces) basil leaves
1/2 cup (2 ounces) grated fresh
   Parmesan cheese
1/4 teaspoon salt

Preparation
1. Turn on food processor. Add nuts and garlic; mince.

2. Add oil; pulse 3 times.

3. Add basil, cheese, and salt; process until finely minced, scraping sides of bowl once.

Nutritional Information: Calories: 64 | Fat: 6 g | Saturated fat: 1 g | Monounsaturated fat: 3 g | Polyunsaturated fat: 1 g | Protein: 3 g | Carbohydrate: 1 g | Fiber: 0 g Cholesterol: 3 mg | Iron: 0.5 mg | Sodium: 134 mg | Calcium: 95 mg

FROM TFK AROUND THE WORLD

Each of Italy's regions has its own special foods. Some regions are known for their cheeses, olives, tomatoes, or meats. Most Italians eat pasta at least once a day. They also enjoy gelato (ice cream), pizza, and espresso (strong coffee).

Know Your Ingredients
Pesto gets its name from *pestle*, as in mortar and pestle, the tools used to grind the sauce's ingredients.

Egg Salad
Sandwich Stacks

The classic club sandwich includes turkey, lettuce, tomatoes, bacon, mayonnaise, and three layers of toasted bread. Here's a meatless version.

Makes: 4 sandwiches

Ingredients

Egg Salad

1/3 cup mayonnaise
4 large hard-boiled eggs, chopped
1 celery stalk, diced
4 bacon slices, cooked and crumbled
1/4 cup chopped fresh chives
1 tablespoon minced sweet onion
1/4 teaspoon seasoned salt
1/2 teaspoon freshly ground pepper

Sandwich

1/3 cup mayonnaise
12 thin white or wheat sandwich bread slices, lightly toasted
1 cup firmly packed fresh spinach

Preparation

Part One: Egg Salad

1. Stir together 1/3 cup mayonnaise, eggs, celery, bacon, chives, onion, salt, and pepper.

Try This
Make a side dish of baked sweet-potato wedges: Cut two sweet potatoes into eight lengthwise wedges each, and rub with canola or olive oil. Spread on a nonstick baking sheet, uncovered, and bake at 350° for 30-45 minutes, or until tender.

Part Two: Sandwich

1. Spread mayonnaise evenly onto one side of each bread slice.

2. Line up 4 bread slices with their mayonnaise sides up.

3. Spread half the egg salad evenly onto each slice.

4. Layer half the spinach evenly among the 4 bread slices.

5. Place 4 more slices of bread on top, mayonnaise side up.

6. Repeat the procedure, alternating another layer of egg salad and of spinach.

7. Top with remaining bread slices, mayonnaise side down.

8. Cut each sandwich into quarters.

Nutritional Information: Calories: 570 | Fat: 40 g | Saturated fat: 8 g | Monounsaturated fat: 10 g | Polyunsaturated fat: 18 g | Protein: 15 g | Carbohydrate: 36 g | Fiber: 2 g Cholesterol: 233 mg | Iron: 2.5 mg | Sodium: 929 mg | Calcium: 191 mg

Smooth and Savory
Cheese Spread

Make this zingy sandwich spread to keep on hand for lunches the whole family will enjoy.

Makes: About 3–1/2 cups (enough for 8 to 10 sandwiches)

Be Safe
Ask an adult to help cook bacon, chop onions, and shred cheese.

Know Your Ingredients
The pimiento (pi-*myen*-toh) is a large, red, heart-shaped chili pepper that is sweet, savory, and aromatic. The word means "pepper" in Spanish.

Ingredients
4 bacon slices
2 (8-ounce) blocks sharp
   cheddar cheese, shredded
1 (4-ounce) jar diced pimientos,
   rinsed and drained
1/2 cup mayonnaise
2 tablespoons finely chopped onion
1 tablespoon Worcestershire sauce
1/4 teaspoon salt
1/8 teaspoon ground red pepper
1/8 teaspoon pepper

Preparation
1. Cook bacon in a large skillet 4 to 5 minutes on each side or until crisp. Remove bacon and drain on paper towels. Crumble bacon.

2. Stir together bacon, cheese, pimientos, mayonnaise, onion, Worcestershire sauce, salt, and both peppers just until blended.

3. Store cheese spread in an airtight container in refrigerator up to 1 week.

Feast on This

Red foods, such as pimientos, add visual interest to a meal. Red vegetables (beets, radishes, sweet red peppers, red onions, red potatoes, tomatoes) make the meal healthy, too. Red beans and kidney beans also contain important nutrients.

Nutritional Information: Calories: 300 | Fat: 22.5 g | Saturated fat: 14 g
Monounsaturated fat: 6 g | Polyunsaturated fat: 1 g | Protein: 13 g | Carbohydrate: 11 g
Fiber: 0.5 g | Cholesterol: 58 mg | Iron: 1 mg | Sodium: 516 mg | Calcium: 349 mg

Soba Noodles with
Sweet & Spicy Shrimp

Cooking the soba noodles takes about six minutes, and you can chop and assemble the remaining ingredients while the noodles cook. Buy peeled, deveined, cooked shrimp, or get raw shrimp and add them to the boiling water a couple of minutes after adding the noodles. This recipe is easily doubled if you need more than one serving.

Makes: 1 serving (serving size: 2 cups)

Ingredients

Soba Noodles

2 ounces uncooked soba (buckwheat) noodles
4 cups water
1/2 cup shredded carrot

Know Your Ingredients
Soba noodles are originally from Japan. They are as thick as spaghetti, and used in many hot and cold dishes.

Shrimp

1 tablespoon rice vinegar
1 teaspoon dark sesame oil
1 teaspoon low-sodium soy sauce
1/4 teaspoon chili-garlic sauce (such as Lee Kum Kee)
1/8 teaspoon sugar
1/2 cup chopped, cooked shrimp (about 3 ounces)
1/4 cup thinly sliced green onions
1 tablespoon chopped fresh cilantro

Preparation

Part One: Soba Noodles

1. Bring 4 cups water to a boil in a medium saucepan. Break noodles in half. Add them to the boiling water and cook 4 minutes.

FROM

TIME
FOR KIDS

Children's Day is a national Japanese holiday in May. The country honors children and mothers. Families raise colorful flags and fly kites with images of carps. The carp is a fish that swims upstream. It stands for strength and determination. People eat *mochi,* which are small cakes made from rice.

2. Add carrot to noodles in pan; cook 2 minutes or until noodles are done. Drain.

Part Two: **Shrimp**

1. Combine vinegar, oil, soy sauce, chili-garlic sauce, and sugar in a medium bowl, stirring with a whisk.

2. Add noodle mixture, shrimp, onions, and cilantro. Toss to coat. Cover and chill.

Nutritional Information: Calories: 357 | Fat: 6 g | Saturated fat: 1 g | Monounsaturated fat: 2.1 g | Polyunsaturated fat: 2.4 g | Protein: 26.9 g | Carbohydrate: 51.7 g | Fiber: 3 g Cholesterol: 166 mg | Iron: 4.7 mg | Sodium: 898 mg | Calcium: 72 mg

Tropical Breeze
Chicken Salad

Serve this salad chilled or at room temperature, depending on your preference. You can substitute lime juice for lemon juice, if you'd like.

Makes: 4 large servings

Ingredients

1 cup uncooked basmati rice

2 cups cubed skinless, boneless rotisserie chicken breast

1 cup cubed fresh pineapple

1 cup jarred sliced, peeled mango, drained and chopped (such as Del Monte SunFresh)

1/2 cup seedless red grapes, halved

1/4 cup sliced almonds, toasted

2 tablespoons finely chopped fresh mint

1-1/2 tablespoons fresh lemon juice

1-1/2 tablespoons canola oil

1/4 teaspoon salt

Preparation

1. Cook rice according to package instructions, omitting salt and fat. Cool.

2. Combine rice, chicken, pineapple, mango, grapes, and almonds in a large bowl.

3. In a small bowl, combine mint, lemon juice, oil, and salt, stirring with a whisk.

Try This

Rotisserie chicken is great to keep on hand for a quick meal. Pick it up at the end of your shopping trip so that it stays hot until you get it home. Serve or refrigerate it within two hours. It'll keep in the refrigerator for three to four days.

4. Drizzle mint dressing over chicken salad; toss well. Cover and chill.

5. Divide chicken salad among 4 bowls.

Nutritional Information: Calories: 346 | Fat: 11.5 g | Saturated fat: 1.4 g | Monounsaturated fat: 6.2 g | Polyunsaturated fat: 3 g | Protein: 25.5 g | Carbohydrate: 36.1 g | Fiber: 2.8 g Cholesterol: 60 mg | Iron: 1.6 mg | Sodium: 199 mg | Calcium: 45 mg

FROM
TIME
FOR KIDS

Still using brown paper lunch sacks? Bag them, many school systems say. They want parents and students to choose reusable cloth sacks instead. This will help schools across the U.S. to have waste-free lunch periods. As schools see it, more students packing their lunches in eco-friendly containers means less waste in the cafeteria.

Cheese Lover's
Grilled Cheese

Love grilled cheese sandwiches? Why not make it a triple! This sandwich grills three types of cheese—provolone, Parmesan, and mozzarella—on slices of Italian bread.

Makes: 4 sandwiches

Ingredients

1/4 cup butter, softened
1 tablespoon grated Parmesan cheese
8 slices Italian bread
4 (3/4-ounce) slices provolone cheese
4 (3/4-ounce) slices mozzarella cheese

Try This
Wrap cheeses loosely. Use waxed or greaseproof paper rather than cling film.

Don't store cheese with other strong-smelling foods; it will absorb other aromas and may spoil.

Let cold cheese warm up for about half an hour before eating to allow the flavor and aroma to develop.

Preparation

1. Preheat a griddle or nonstick skillet on medium heat.

2. Stir together butter and Parmesan cheese in a small bowl.

3. Spread 1-1/2 teaspoons of the butter-cheese mixture on one side of each bread slice.

4. Place 4 bread slices on waxed paper, buttered sides down.

5. Top each bread slice with a slice of provolone cheese and a slice of mozzarella cheese.

6. Top each with the remaining bread slices, buttered sides up.

7. Cook sandwiches, in batches, on the preheated griddle or nonstick skillet, gently pressing with a spatula. Cook for 4 minutes on each side or until golden brown and cheese is melted.

Nutritional Information: Calories: 300 | Fat: 22.5 g | Saturated fat: 14 g | Monounsaturated fat: 6 g | Polyunsaturated fat: 1 g | Protein: 13 g | Carbohydrate: 11 g | Fiber: 0.5 g Cholesterol: 58 mg | Iron: 1 mg | Sodium: 516 mg | Calcium: 349 mg

Cheese Producers

The U.S. is the world's top cheese maker (more than 10 billion pounds in 2010). Here are the five countries that produce the most cheese:

1. United States
2. Germany
3. France
4. Italy
5. Netherlands

Source: "Total and Retail Cheese Consumption," Canadian Dairy Information Centre; dairyinfo.gc.ca

Life of the Party
Pizza Sticks

Jarred bruschetta topping, chock-full of flavorful herbs and veggies, saves both money and prep time for these cheesy pizza sticks. The store-bought shredded cheese and refrigerated pizza crust also help make this a quick and easy lunch.

Makes: about 12 pizza sticks

Feast on This

Italy gets most of the credit for inventing pizza, but some attribute the invention to Persian soldiers, who around 500 B.C. baked a flatbread on their shields and used cheese and dates as toppings.

Ingredients

1 (12-ounce) refrigerated thin pizza crust
1 (10-1/2-ounce) container tomato bruschetta topping
1 cup (4 ounces) shredded Italian cheese blend

Preparation

1. Preheat oven to 450°.

2. Top pizza crust with bruschetta topping and sprinkle evenly with cheese.

3. Bake directly on oven rack for 12 minutes or until crust is golden and cheese is bubbly.

4. Cut pizza in half, then cut each half lengthwise into 2-inch-wide strips.

Nutritional Information: Calories: 131 | Fat: 5 g | Saturated fat: 1.3 g | Monounsaturated fat: 2.2 g | Polyunsaturated fat: 0.65 g | Protein: 5 g | Carbohydrate: 15 g | Fiber: 0.5 g Cholesterol: 3 mg | Iron: 0.6 mg | Sodium: 323 mg | Calcium: 67.5 mg

FROM TFK AROUND THE WORLD

Besides culinary delights, Italy has a wealth of cultural treasures. Ancient Romans built great stone temples and beautiful monuments. During the Renaissance (1300–1600 A.D.)— a period of renewed interest in culture— talented composers, writers, artists, and architects created masterpieces that continue to inspire people today.

Speak Italian

Barbecue Chicken
Picnic Sandwich

Barbecuing has become an American pastime and just about every family has its own special recipe for barbecue sauce to slather on chicken, ribs, or steak. Some are sweet and others are spicy. Try our version for your next picnic.

Makes: 6 sandwiches

Ingredients

Chicken

1/2 cup no-salt-added ketchup
2 tablespoons honey mustard
2 tablespoons water
3/4 teaspoon ancho chili powder
3/4 teaspoon smoked paprika
1/2 teaspoon garlic powder
1/2 teaspoon onion powder
1/2 teaspoon ground cumin
1/2 teaspoon Worcestershire sauce
1/8 teaspoon kosher salt
3 cups shredded skinless, boneless rotisserie chicken

Coleslaw

3 tablespoons canola mayonnaise
2 tablespoons cider vinegar
1 teaspoon sugar
3 cups packaged coleslaw
1/3 cup chopped green onions

Sandwich

6 hamburger buns, toasted

Know Your Ingredients
Cumin is the second most popular spice in the world, after black pepper.

Try This
Make and refrigerate the chicken and coleslaw mixtures the night before, and in the morning you'll make lunch in minutes!

Preparation

Part One: Chicken

1. In a saucepan, combine ketchup, mustard, water, chili powder, paprika, garlic powder, onion powder, cumin, Worcestershire sauce, and salt. Bring to a simmer. Cook 10 minutes.

2. Combine sauce with chicken in a large bowl.

Part Two: Coleslaw

1. In a large bowl, combine mayonnaise, vinegar, and sugar.

2. Add coleslaw and onions; toss.

Part Three: Sandwich

1. Place bottom halves of toasted buns in a row. Divide chicken mixture evenly among them.

2. Evenly divide coleslaw mixture among sandwiches.

3. Place top bun on each.

Nutritional Information: Calories: 316 | Fat: 9.9 g | Saturated fat: 1.5 g | Monounsaturated fat: 4.3 g | Polyunsaturated fat: 2.7 g | Protein: 21.4 g | Carbohydrate: 35.3 g | Fiber: 2.1 g
Cholesterol: 53 mg | Iron: 2.1 mg | Sodium: 548 mg | Calcium: 91 mg

FROM TIME FOR KIDS

Kids' lunches that are stored in cubbies, lockers, desks, or closets often don't maintain a safe temperature. Next time you bring lunch to school, add extra ice packs to the bag or make sure it gets refrigerated.

Cheesy Roll-Up
Pigs in Blankets

Pigs in blankets aren't cold farm animals. They're tasty treats, and these are not even made from pork!

Makes: 4 servings (serving size: 2 pigs in blankets)

Ingredients

The Blankets

1 (6-ounce) portion fresh pizza dough
1-1/2 ounces part-skim mozzarella cheese, shredded

The Pigs

4 turkey hot dogs, halved crosswise
Cooking spray

Special Dipping Sauce

2 tablespoons ketchup
1 tablespoon barbecue sauce
1 teaspoon prepared mustard

Preparation

Part One: **The Blankets**

1. Preheat oven to 425°.

2. Let dough stand, covered, for 20 minutes. On a lightly floured surface, roll the dough into a rectangle, 12 inches long and 4 inches wide.

3. Cut the dough into 4 smaller rectangles.

4. Cut each of these rectangles in half diagonally to form 8 triangles.

5. Divide cheese evenly among dough triangles, placing it in the center of the wider ends.

Part Two: **The Pigs**

1. Place a hot-dog half at the wide end of each triangle and roll it up toward the small end, pinching the ends to seal. Repeat until all are prepared.

2. Coat baking sheet with cooking spray. Arrange rolls on the baking sheet and bake in preheated oven for 12 minutes.

Part Three: **Special Dipping Sauce**

1. Combine ketchup, barbecue sauce, and mustard.

Nutritional Information: Calories: 215 | Fat: 6.4 g | Saturated fat: 2.1 g | Monounsaturated fat: 0.5 g | Polyunsaturated fat: 0.8 g | Protein: 13.5 g | Carbohydrate: 27.5 g | Fiber: 0.8 g Cholesterol: 32 mg | Iron: 1.4 mg | Sodium: 825 mg | Calcium: 85 mg

Soup-er Quick
Chicken Noodle Soup

Heat the broth mixture in the microwave to jump-start the cooking. While the broth mixture heats, sauté the aromatic ingredients in your soup pot to get this dish under way. Though we like the spiral shape of fusilli, you can also make this soup with rotini or orzo.

Makes: 6 servings (serving size: about 1 cup)

Feast on This
Four towns in the U.S. have the word *chicken* in their name: Chicken, Alaska; Chicken Bristle, Illinois; Chicken Bristle, Kentucky; and Chickentown, Pennsylvania.

Ingredients
2 cups water
1 (32-ounce) carton fat-free, lower-sodium chicken broth
1 tablespoon olive oil
1/2 cup chopped onion
1/2 cup chopped celery
1 medium carrot, chopped
1/2 teaspoon salt
1/2 teaspoon freshly ground black pepper
6 ounces fusilli
2-1/2 cups shredded skinless, boneless rotisserie chicken breast
2 tablespoons chopped fresh flat-leaf parsley

Preparation
1. Combine water and chicken broth in a microwave-safe dish, and microwave on high for 5 minutes.

2. While broth mixture heats, heat a large saucepan over medium-high heat. Add oil to pan; swirl to coat.

3. Add onion, celery, carrot, salt, and pepper; sauté 3 minutes or until almost tender.

4. Add hot broth mixture and pasta; bring to a boil.

sauté (saw-*tay*) to cook food in a pan with a small amount of oil, butter, or other fat

FROM TFK AROUND THE WORLD

Each day, 120 million children across India are given the energy they need to focus on learning. A special school lunch program allows them to eat unlimited helpings as long as they finish what's on their plates. In one town, school attendance increased 12%. The number of underweight children dropped 12%, too.

5. Cook 7 minutes or until pasta is almost al dente. Stir in chicken; cook 1 minute or until thoroughly heated.

6. Stir in parsley.

Nutritional Information: Calories: 231 | Fat: 4.9 g | Saturated fat: 0.9 g | Monounsaturated fat: 2.4 g | Polyunsaturated fat: 0.7 g | Protein: 21.7 g | Carbohydrate: 23.6 g | Fiber: 1.7 g Cholesterol: 50 mg | Iron: 1.4 mg | Sodium: 586 mg | Calcium: 31 mg

al dente (all-*den*-tay) the texture of cooked pasta when it is soft but still a bit firm inside; in Italian, this phrase means "to the teeth"

FROM

TIME
FOR KIDS

Not all soups are considered legal. To protect the world's dwindling shark population, shark-fin soup is banned in several U.S. states. A delicacy in some Asian cultures, shark-fin soup is often served at weddings and special events.

puree (pure-*ay*) to blend cooked food until it's creamy, as in a dip or a soup

Creamy Tomato
Alphabet Soup

On chilly autumn afternoons, nothing warms more than a good bowl of creamy tomato soup and a grilled cheese sandwich. Pureed alphabet pasta, instead of cream, thickens the soup in this version.

Makes: 6 servings (serving size: about 1 cup)

Ingredients

2 tablespoons butter
1 cup chopped onion
1 cup chopped carrot
1/2 cup chopped celery
1-1/2 cups vegetable broth
1 teaspoon dried basil
1/4 teaspoon black pepper
1 (28-ounce) can diced tomatoes, undrained
2 cups cooked alphabet pasta (about 1 cup uncooked pasta), divided
1 cup 2% reduced-fat milk

Preparation

1. Melt the butter in a saucepan over medium-high heat. Add onion, carrot, and celery; sauté 4 minutes or until tender.

2. Add broth, basil, pepper, and tomatoes, and bring to a boil. Reduce heat; simmer 15 minutes.

3. Stir in 1/2 cup pasta. Remove from heat; let stand 5 minutes.

4. Place half the tomato mixture in a blender, and process until smooth. Pour pureed soup into a large bowl.

5. Repeat procedure with remaining tomato mixture. Return pureed soup to pan; stir in remaining pasta and milk.

6. Cook over medium-high heat 2 minutes or until thoroughly heated, stirring frequently (do not boil).

Feast on This

Why do we "eat" rather than "drink" soup? It may be because soup is considered part of the meal. And in most cultures, soup is consumed with a spoon, rather than sipped from the container.

Nutritional Information: Calories: 175 | Fat: 5.2 g | Saturated fat: 2.9 g | Monounsaturated fat: 1.3 g | Polyunsaturated fat: 0.2 g | Protein: 6.1 g | Carbohydrate: 27.9 g | Fiber: 4 g Cholesterol: 13 mg | Iron: 1.3 mg | Sodium: 492 mg | Calcium: 93 mg

Mangia!
Margherita Panini

Panini are pressed sandwiches. A small appliance called a panini press is available in stores, but a heavy skillet placed on the sandwiches as they cook works just as well. You can even weigh down a lighter skillet with canned goods or a brick wrapped in foil.

Makes: 4 sandwiches

Feast on This

This dish takes its name from the Margherita pizza, named for Queen Margherita of Italy. During her 1889 visit to Naples, in her honor, a pizza was prepared to resemble the Italian flag: red (tomato), white (mozzarella), and green (basil).

Ingredients

8 (1-inch-thick) slices rustic French bread loaf
16 (1/8-inch-thick) slices plum tomato (2 large tomatoes)
1/4 teaspoon salt
1/4 teaspoon freshly ground black pepper
1 cup (4 ounces) shredded part-skim mozzarella cheese
12 fresh basil leaves
8 teaspoons extra-virgin olive oil
1/4 cup melted butter, divided

Preparation

1. Place 4 bread slices in a row; divide tomato slices evenly among them and sprinkle evenly with salt and pepper. Sprinkle cheese over tomatoes.

2. Arrange basil leaves evenly over cheese, and top with remaining bread slices. Drizzle 1 teaspoon olive oil over top of each sandwich.

3. Heat a grill pan or large nonstick skillet over medium-high heat until hot. Place sandwiches in pan, oil sides down. Drizzle 1 teaspoon oil over top of each sandwich. Brush the pan with 2 tablespoons of the butter.

4. Put a piece of foil over sandwiches in pan; place a heavy skillet on top of foil to press sandwiches.

5. Using tongs, carefully remove the foil and flip the sandwiches. Put foil and skillet back on top of sandwiches. Cook 2 minutes or until golden brown. Serve immediately.

Nutritional Information: Calories: 320 | Fat: 16 g | Saturated fat: 3 g | Monounsaturated fat: 9 g
Polyunsaturated fat: 4 g | Protein: 12 g | Carbohydrate: 31 g | Fiber: 1.5 g | Cholesterol: 0 mg
Iron: 2 mg | Sodium: 532 mg | Calcium: 47 mg

Olive-Oil Producers
Spain makes more olive oil than Italy and Greece combined. Here are the world's top olive-oil producers:
1. Spain
2. Italy
3. Greece
4. Syria
5. Turkey

Source: *TIME FOR KIDS Around the World: Greece*

Mouthwatering
Monte Cristo Sandwich

When not just any sandwich will do, get adventurous and try making this variation on the classic Monte Cristo. This special lunch traces its origins to a hot ham-and-cheese sandwich first served in French cafes 100 years ago.

Makes: 2 sandwiches

Ingredients

4 (1-ounce) slices white bread
2 teaspoons Dijon mustard
3 ounces (1/4-inch-thick) sliced deli turkey
2 ounces reduced-fat Swiss cheese or
    Jarlsberg cheese, thinly sliced
1 medium tomato, thinly sliced
1/8 teaspoon freshly ground black pepper
1 large egg
1 large egg white
1 tablespoon 1% low-fat milk
1-1/2 tablespoons chopped fresh basil
Cooking spray
1/2 teaspoon butter

Preparation

1. Spread mustard evenly onto one side of each bread slice.

2. Divide turkey, cheese, and tomato slices evenly between 2 slices of bread. Sprinkle with pepper and top with remaining bread slices, mustard side down.

3. Combine egg, egg white, milk, and basil in a shallow dish; stir well with a whisk.

Be Safe
Use tongs to carefully dip and thoroughly coat sandwiches in the egg mixture. Once you've prepared the sandwiches, have an adult help cook them.

Feast on This
In the original version of the Monte Cristo sandwich, a grilled ham-and-cheese meets French toast, complete with drizzled maple syrup.

4. Coat a large nonstick skillet with cooking spray and place over medium heat until hot. Add butter.

5. Dip both sides of each sandwich into egg mixture and place in pan. Cook 3 to 4 minutes on each side or until cheese melts and sandwiches are golden.

6. Cut sandwiches in half, and serve immediately.

Nutritional Information: Calories: 364 | Fat: 12 g | Saturated fat: 4.5 g | Monounsaturated fat: 3 g | Polyunsaturated fat: 1.4 g | Protein: 29.5 g | Carbohydrate: 33 g | Fiber: 2 g Cholesterol: 137 mg | Iron: 3 mg | Sodium: 833 mg | Calcium: 390 mg

CHAPTER 3

Sides and Snacks

Snack attacks can happen anytime, day or night. Satisfy your craving for "just a little something" with these recipes. Many can be served as side dishes as well. Pair one with your favorite lunch or dinner recipe. Presto! You've got a complete meal.

- On the Go Munchies Mix
- Oatmeal-Raisin Energizer Bars
- Coconut + Fruit + Sushi Rice = Frushi
- Roasted Sweet-Potato Fries
- Tangy, Cheesy Broccoli Trees

And many more yummy treats!

Yummm-kin
Pumpkin Dip

Know Your Ingredients
Be sure to purchase 100% pure pumpkin and not pumpkin-pie filling.

FROM

FOR KIDS

Chris Stevens squashed the competition at the 2010 Stillwater Harvest Fest and Giant Pumpkin Weigh-Off, in Minnesota. His world-record-breaking pumpkin tipped the scales at just over 1,800 pounds.

Crunchy foods on the sweeter side taste even better when dunked in this tasty dip.

Makes: **8 servings (serving size: 1/4 cup)**

Ingredients
3/4 cup 1/3-less-fat cream cheese, softened
1/4 cup packed brown sugar
1/2 cup canned pumpkin
1 tablespoon maple syrup
1/2 teaspoon ground
    cinnamon

Preparation
1. Combine cream cheese, brown sugar, and pumpkin in a medium bowl. Beat with a mixer at medium speed until well combined.

2. Add syrup and cinnamon, and beat until smooth.

3. Cover and chill 30 minutes before serving.

4. Enjoy this dip with peeled apple slices or cinnamon pita chips.

Nutritional Information: Calories: 91 | Fat: 4.6 g | Saturated fat: 3.1 g | Monounsaturated fat: 0 g | Polyunsaturated fat: 0 g | Protein: 2.5 g | Carbohydrate: 10.5 g | Fiber: 0.5 g
Cholesterol: 15 mg | Iron: 0.4 mg | Sodium: 135 mg | Calcium: 28 mg

Creamy
Ranch Dip

Serve this dip with all sorts of crisp and crunchy vegetables.

Makes: **6 servings (serving size: about 2 tablespoons)**

Ingredients

1/2 cup 1/3-less-fat cream cheese,
  softened
3 tablespoons nonfat buttermilk
2 tablespoons chopped fresh flat-leaf parsley
1 teaspoon chopped fresh dill
1/2 teaspoon minced fresh garlic
1/4 teaspoon onion powder
1/4 teaspoon salt
1/4 teaspoon freshly ground
  black pepper

Preparation

1. Combine cream cheese and buttermilk in a small bowl, stirring with a whisk until blended.

2. Stir in parsley, dill, garlic, onion powder, salt, and pepper.

3. Serve this dip with baby carrots, broccoli florets, or other fresh vegetables.

Feast on This
Thanks to lactic acid, buttermilk is tart and thick and keeps easily for weeks in your refrigerator. Acid is a natural preservative because it inhibits the growth of disease-causing bacteria.

Nutritional Information: Calories: 52 | Fat: 4.3 g
Saturated fat: 2.4 g | Monounsaturated fat: 1.1 g
Polyunsaturated fat: 0.2 g | Protein: 2.1 g
Carbohydrate: 1.4 g | Fiber: 0.1 g | Cholesterol: 14 mg
Iron: 0.1 mg | Sodium: 170 mg | Calcium: 34 mg

Protein-Packed
Peanut Dip

You can also use this dip as a protein-rich spread for veggie wraps or sandwiches made with grated carrot, sliced cucumber, and lettuce.

Know Your Ingredients

Peanut butter contains lots of protein and mostly heart-healthy fat. Choose peanut butter that's labeled "natural"—it has much less added sugar, salt, and trans-fatty acids.

Makes: 8 servings (serving size: 2 tablespoons)

Ingredients

1/2 cup natural creamy peanut butter
1/3 cup reduced-fat, firm silken tofu
3 tablespoons brown sugar
2 tablespoons fresh lime juice
2 tablespoons low-sodium
    soy sauce
1 garlic clove,
    crushed

Preparation

1. Place peanut butter, tofu, brown sugar, lime juice, soy sauce, and garlic in a blender; process until smooth.

2. Serve the dip with pea pods, cucumber halves, sugar snap peas, carrot sticks, and broccoli florets.

3. Store in an airtight container in refrigerator for up to 2 days.

Nutritional Information: Calories: 122 | Fat: 7.7 g | Saturated fat: 1.5 g | Monounsaturated fat: 3.8 g | Polyunsaturated fat: 2.5 g | Protein: 5.4 g | Carbohydrate: 7.4 g | Fiber: 0.5 g Cholesterol: 0 mg | Iron: 0.4 mg | Sodium: 131 mg | Calcium: 19 mg

On the Go
Munchies Mix

SIMPLE

This snack travels well, so you can bring these munchies to your next party, sports event, or trip to Grandma's house.

Makes: **35 servings (serving size: 1 cup)**

Ingredients

5 cups rice-cereal squares
2 (12.6-ounce) bags candy-coated chocolate pieces
1 (16-ounce) bag mini pretzel twists
1 (13.7-ounce) package bite-size Parmesan-and-garlic crackers
1 (12-ounce) container honey-roasted peanuts

Try This
Like sweet and salty together? Try corn chips with a banana, or potato chips with chocolate.

Preparation
1. Combine cereal, chocolate, pretzels, crackers, and peanuts in a large bowl.

2. Store in an airtight container for up to 2 weeks.

Nutritional Information:
Calories: 277 | Fat: 12 g
Saturated fat: 4 g
Monounsaturated fat: 4.26 g
Polyunsaturated fat: 2.95 g
Protein: 5 g | Carbohydrate: 38 g
Fiber: 1.5 g | Cholesterol: 3 mg
Iron: 3 mg | Sodium: 415 mg
Calcium: 43 mg

Incredible Edible
Nutty Putty

Peanuts are a good source of protein and B vitamins, nutrients that help to keep your brain sharp. The best part about this recipe: It's food you can play with!

Makes: 24 servings

(serving size: 1 tablespoon)

Ingredients
1 cup creamy peanut butter
3 tablespoons honey
1 cup instant nonfat dry milk
Decorations (optional): Raisins, colored sugar, candy sprinkles

Preparation
1. Stir together peanut butter and honey in a big bowl. Add dry milk, stirring until blended.

2. Spoon a small amount onto a plate. Shape and decorate it by hand, anyway you wish, before gobbling it up.

3. Store remaining putty in the refrigerator in an airtight container for up to 1 week.

Nutritional Information: Calories: 81 | Fat: 5.3 g | Saturated fat: 1 g | Monounsaturated fat: 0 g | Polyunsaturated fat: 0 g | Protein: 3.7 g | Carbohydrate: 6 g | Fiber: 0.7 g Cholesterol: 0 mg | Iron: 0.3 mg | Sodium: 66 mg | Calcium: 38 mg

Make Mine Marshmallow
Nice Crispy Bars

Long before it was whipped into gooey goodness, the marshmallow plant was sometimes used for medicinal purposes. This updated favorite snack will make anyone feel better!

Makes: **24 bars**

Ingredients
3 tablespoons butter
1 (10-1/2-ounce) bag
    miniature marshmallows
1 (15-ounce) box multigrain
    cluster cereal
1 cup dried cranberries
    plus 1/4 cup
Cooking spray

Preparation
1. Melt butter in a large saucepan over low heat. Add marshmallows, and cook, stirring constantly, 4 to 5 minutes or until melted and smooth. Remove from heat.

2. Stir in cereal and 1 cup cranberries until well coated.

3. Coat 13-by-9-inch baking dish with cooking spray and press mixture into dish. Chop remaining cranberries, and sprinkle on top.

4. Let stand 10 to 15 minutes or until firm. Cut into 24 bars.

Try This
You can store the bars in a pan or on a plate, covered. Or put them in sealable sandwich bags for midday snack attacks.

Nutritional Information: Calories: 132 | Fat: 1.9 g | Saturated fat: 0.9 g
Monounsaturated fat: 0.4 g | Polyunsaturated fat: 0.1 g | Protein: 2.6 g | Carbohydrate: 27.6 g
Fiber: 1.7 g | Cholesterol: 4 mg | Iron: 0.6 mg | Sodium: 22 mg | Calcium: 8 mg

Oatmeal-Raisin
Energizer Bars

Here's an awesome power bar you can make on your own. It's easy to throw in your bag on the way to sports practice or dance rehearsal.

Makes: **28 bars**

Know Your Ingredients
Brown sugar is made by refining sugar cane, then adding some of the molasses extracted during refinement back to the white sugar.

Ingredients
1/4 cup chilled butter or stick margarine, cut into small pieces
2/3 cup packed brown sugar
3 cups regular oats
1 cup raisins
1/2 cup dried cranberries
1/2 cup chopped dried apricots
1 teaspoon ground cinnamon
1/4 teaspoon ground nutmeg
2 large egg whites, lightly beaten
1/2 cup chunky peanut butter
1/2 cup fat-free sweetened condensed milk
Cooking spray

Preparation

1. Preheat oven to 350°.

2. In a large bowl, cut butter into brown sugar with a pastry blender until crumbly. Stir in oats, raisins, cranberries, apricots, cinnamon, and nutmeg.

3. Combine egg whites, peanut butter, and condensed milk in a small bowl; stir with a whisk until smooth. Add egg mixture to oats, and stir well.

**Feast
on This**
Like most athletes, dancers need to pay attention to good nutrition. Their classes, rehearsals, and performances require lots of energy. A dancer's diet should consist of a balance of carbohydrates, proteins, fats, vitamins, minerals, and fluids.

4. Press mixture into a jelly-roll pan coated with cooking spray. Bake in oven for 20 minutes.

5. Cool completely. Cut into 28 bars.

Nutritional Information: Calories: 141 | Fat: 5 g | Saturated fat: 1.5 g | Monounsaturated fat: 1.8 g | Polyunsaturated fat: 1 g | Protein: 3 g | Carbohydrate: 23 g | Fiber: 2 g Cholesterol: 5 mg | Iron: 1 mg | Sodium: 46 mg | Calcium: 27 mg

Coconut + Fruit + Sushi Rice =
Frushi

Frushi (fruit sushi) is a fun snack that gets everyone involved. It makes a festive treat for a birthday party or a sleepover with friends.

Makes: **5 servings (serving size: 4 frushi pieces)**

Know Your Ingredients
Coconut is high in saturated fat, so avoid eating it too often.

Try This
If the fruit won't stick to the rice, use a dab of honey to help "glue" it. This recipe calls for oranges and raspberries for toppings, but any fresh fruit will work, especially ripe mangoes.

Ingredients
1-1/4 cups water
1 cup uncooked sushi rice or other short-grain rice
1/4 cup sugar
1/4 cup light coconut milk
Dash of salt
Cooking spray
10 orange sections
20 fresh raspberries
1 (6-ounce) carton vanilla fat-free yogurt

Preparation
1. Bring water and rice to a boil in a medium saucepan. Cover, reduce heat, and simmer 15 minutes or until water is almost absorbed. Remove from heat; let stand, covered, 15 minutes.

2. Place rice in a large bowl. Add sugar, coconut milk, and salt, stirring gently until well combined. Cover and let stand 20 minutes.

3. Line a baking sheet with waxed paper. Lightly coat hands with cooking spray. Divide rice mixture into 20 equal portions, shaping each into a ball (about 1 rounded tablespoon each). Lightly press each rice ball into an oval between palms; place ovals on lined baking sheet. (If your hands become sticky, you may have to wash your hands and coat them again.)

4. Top 10 rice ovals with 1 orange section each, pressing gently so that it sticks. Top remaining ovals with 2 raspberries each.

5. Cover and chill frushi until ready to serve. Serve with yogurt for dipping.

Feast on This

Sushi is a finger food from Japan typically made with rice, raw fish, and other savory ingredients. Its popularity has spread throughout the world.

Nutritional Information: Calories: 228 | Fat: 1 g | Saturated fat: 0.7 g
Monounsaturated fat: 0.1 g | Polyunsaturated fat: 0.1 g | Protein: 4.2 g | Carbohydrate: 50.2 g
Fiber: 1.4 g | Cholesterol: 1 mg | Iron: 0.4 mg | Sodium: 53 mg | Calcium: 71 mg

Summertime Broccoli
Slaw Salad

No barbecue is complete without coleslaw. Broccoli slaw is a vibrant-green twist on the classic cabbage version.

Makes: 6 servings (serving size: 3/4 cup)

Ingredients

4 center-cut bacon slices
1/3 cup light mayonnaise
2 tablespoons plain fat-free yogurt
2 teaspoons cider vinegar
1 teaspoon sugar
1/4 teaspoon salt
1/4 teaspoon freshly ground black pepper
1 (12-ounce) package broccoli slaw
1/2 cup finely chopped red onion
1/2 cup raisins
2 tablespoons chopped pecans, toasted

Nutritional Information: Calories: 150 | Fat: 7 g | Saturated fat: 1.5 g | Monounsaturated fat: 2.6 g | Polyunsaturated fat: 2.6 g Protein: 4 g | Carbohydrate: 18 g | Fiber: 2.7 g | Cholesterol: 10 mg Iron: 1 mg | Sodium: 320 mg | Calcium: 33 mg

Preparation

1. Cook bacon in a large nonstick skillet over medium heat until crisp. Remove bacon from pan; crumble and set aside.

2. Combine mayonnaise, yogurt, vinegar, sugar, salt, and pepper in a bowl.

3. Add broccoli slaw, onion, and raisins; toss to coat.

4. Cover and chill until ready to serve. Sprinkle with bacon and pecans before serving.

Feast on This

California produces about 95% of the broccoli grown commercially in the United States. The second-biggest producer is Arizona.

Toasted Mozzarella
Cheese Poppers

Make these lip-smackin' cheese poppers for a quick snack.

Makes: **4 servings (serving size: 3 poppers)**

Ingredients
1/3 cup panko bread crumbs
3 tablespoons egg substitute
3 (1-ounce) sticks part-skim mozzarella string cheese
Cooking spray
1/4 cup lower-sodium marinara sauce (such as McCutcheon's)

Preparation

1. Preheat oven to 425°.

2. Heat a medium-size skillet over medium heat. Add panko to pan, and cook for 2 minutes or until toasted, stirring frequently. Remove pan from heat, and place the panko in a shallow dish.

3. Put egg substitute in a shallow dish.

4. Cut each mozzarella stick into 4 equal-size pieces. Working with one piece at a time, dip cheese in egg substitute; then press it into the panko, coating all sides.

5. Coat a baking sheet with cooking spray. Place poppers on sheet and bake in oven for 3 minutes or until the cheese is softened and thoroughly heated.

6. Pour marinara sauce into a microwave-safe bowl. Microwave on high for 1 minute or until thoroughly heated, stirring after 30 seconds.

7. Serve mozzarella pieces with marinara sauce.

Know Your Ingredients
Authentic Italian mozzarella cheese is made with water-buffalo milk.

The biggest difference between panko, or Japanese bread crumbs, and standard bread crumbs is that panko is made from bread without crusts. The flakes tend to stay crispier longer because they don't absorb as much cooking oil.

Nutritional Information: Calories: 91 | Fat: 5.1 g | Saturated fat: 2.8 g
Monounsaturated fat: 1.3 g | Polyunsaturated fat: 0.3 g | Protein: 7.2 g | Carbohydrate: 6.7 g
Fiber: 0.1 g | Cholesterol: 12 mg | Iron: 0.3 mg | Sodium: 162 mg | Calcium: 162 mg

Roasted
Sweet-Potato Fries

Just one serving of sweet potatoes can provide you with as much as 700% of the U.S. Recommended Daily Allowance for vitamin A. Enjoy this totally-good-for-you side dish!

Makes: **6 servings (serving size: 4 wedges)**

Ingredients

4 medium sweet potatoes (about 2-1/2 pounds), scrubbed, each cut into 6 wedges
1 tablespoon chopped fresh rosemary
2 tablespoons olive oil
1 teaspoon salt
1 teaspoon freshly ground black pepper
1/2 teaspoon garlic powder
Cooking spray

Preparation

1. Preheat oven to 450°.

2. Combine potato wedges, rosemary, olive oil, salt, pepper, and garlic powder in a large bowl; toss well.

3. Coat a roasting pan with cooking spray. Arrange potatoes in a single layer. Bake in oven for 20 minutes. Gently stir potatoes, and bake an additional 10 minutes or until lightly browned and tender.

Nutritional Information: Calories: 109 | Fat: 4.5 g | Saturated fat: 0.6 g
Monounsaturated fat: 3.3 g | Polyunsaturated fat: 0.48 g | Protein: 1.5 g | Carbohydrate: 16 g
Fiber: 3 g | Cholesterol: 0 mg | Iron: 0.5 mg | Sodium: 440 mg | Calcium: 16 mg

Be Safe

How to safely cut a sweet potato: Cut the potato in half, the long way, pressing down on the non-sharp side of the knife with the palm of your other hand. Place the flat sides of the potato face-down on your cutting board, and cut slices the long way again. Cut the slices crosswise if you want smaller pieces for fries.

Cheesy Chive
Potato Chips

No one says no to homemade potato chips. And since the white potato has all the essential vitamins except for vitamin A, this snack is healthy, too.

Makes: **7 servings (serving size: 9 to 10 chips)**

Ingredients

1 (12-ounce) baking potato
1 tablespoon olive oil
3 tablespoons grated fresh
   Parmesan cheese
3 tablespoons minced fresh chives
3/4 teaspoon salt
Cooking spray

Preparation

1. Preheat oven to 400°.

2. Scrub potato with a brush. Cut potato lengthwise into very thin slices.

3. Combine potato slices and oil in a large bowl. Add cheese, chives, and salt, and toss gently to coat.

4. Coat baking sheets with cooking spray. Arrange potato slices in a single layer. Bake in oven for 18 to 20 minutes or until golden.

Try This
Chips will brown at different rates. Watch them carefully, and quickly remove individual chips from the oven as they become golden.

Nutritional Information: Calories: 70 | Fat: 2.6 g | Saturated fat: 0.7 g | Monounsaturated fat: 1.6 g | Polyunsaturated fat: 0.23 g | Protein: 2 g | Carbohydrate: 10 g | Fiber: 1 g Cholesterol: 2 mg | Iron: 0.6 mg | Sodium: 294 mg | Calcium: 35 mg

Brown and Green
Buttered Beans

Browning butter is a French technique that gives butter a rich and nutty flavor. Perfect for spiffing up green beans!

Makes: **4 servings (serving size: about 1 cup)**

Ingredients
3 tablespoons butter
1 garlic clove, minced
1 pound fresh green beans, trimmed
1/2 small sweet onion, sliced
1/2 teaspoon salt
1/4 teaspoon freshly ground pepper

Preparation
1. Microwave butter in a 2-cup glass measuring cup on high for 1-1/2 to 2 minutes or until butter is brown.

2. Remove from microwave, and immediately add minced garlic.

3. Place green beans, onion, and 3 tablespoons water in a microwave-safe bowl. Cover bowl tightly with plastic wrap, folding back a small edge to allow steam to escape.

4. Microwave beans on high for 4 to 5 minutes or until vegetables are tender; drain.

5. Toss together bean and brown butter mixtures, and salt. Sprinkle with pepper.

Nutritional Information: Calories: 119 | Fat: 9 g | Saturated fat: 5.5 g | Monounsaturated fat: 2 g | Polyunsaturated fat: 0.5 g | Protein: 3 g | Carbohydrate: 10 g | Fiber: 4 g Cholesterol: 23 mg | Iron: 1 mg | Sodium: 364 mg | Calcium: 50 mg

Tangy, Cheesy
Broccoli Trees

Serve a side forest of broccoli "trees." Broccoli is packed full of fiber, minerals, and vitamins A, B, and C.

MODERATE

Makes: 6 servings (serving size: 2/3 cup)

Ingredients

5 cups raw broccoli florets
2 tablespoons extra-virgin
    olive oil
2 garlic cloves, chopped
1/2 teaspoon grated lemon rind
1 teaspoon fresh lemon juice
1/4 teaspoon kosher salt
3 tablespoons shaved Parmesan cheese
Toasted pine nuts for garnish (optional)

Know Your Ingredients
Broccoli is a member of the cruciferous family of vegetables. Cruciferous plants have flowers with four petals in the shape of a cross. This group includes cabbage, cauliflower, and brussels sprouts.

Preparation

1. Arrange broccoli in a steamer.

2. Steam, covered, 4 minutes or until crisp-tender. Place broccoli in a large bowl.

3. Heat a small skillet over medium-high heat.

4. Add oil and garlic; cook 2 minutes or until garlic is fragrant.

5. Add oil mixture, lemon rind, lemon juice, and salt to broccoli; toss to coat.

6. Sprinkle broccoli with Parmesan cheese.

Nutritional Information: Calories: 71 | Fat: 5.7 g | Saturated fat: 1.2 g
Monounsaturated fat: 3.3 g | Polyunsaturated fat: 0.6 g | Protein: 2.9 g | Carbohydrate: 3.5 g
Fiber: 1.7 g | Cholesterol: 3 mg | Iron: 0.5 mg | Sodium: 146 mg | Calcium: 67 mg

Tasty Lemon–Sage
Spaghetti Squash

This special squash's long strands look like spaghetti when cooked. Serve it as a savory side dish instead of pasta or rice.

Makes: 6 servings (serving size: 1/2 cup)

Know Your Ingredients
Many people think squash is a vegetable, but it's actually a fruit.

Ingredients
1 (2-pound) spaghetti squash
1/3 cup water
2 tablespoons light stick butter
1/4 cup chopped onion
2 garlic cloves, minced
2 tablespoons shredded Parmesan cheese
2 teaspoons small fresh sage leaves
1 teaspoon grated lemon rind
1/2 teaspoon salt
1/4 teaspoon freshly ground black pepper

Preparation
1. Pierce squash several times with a fork; place in an 11-by-7-inch baking dish. Microwave, uncovered, on high for 6 minutes.

2. Cut squash in half lengthwise; discard seeds.

3. Place squash, cut sides up, in baking dish; add water to the dish. Cover dish tightly with plastic wrap, folding back a small edge to allow steam to escape.

4. Microwave on high for 5 minutes or until tender. Drain and cool 15 minutes.

5. While squash cools, melt butter in a large nonstick skillet over medium-high heat. Add onion and garlic; sauté 2 to 3 minutes or until onion is tender.

6. Using a fork, remove spaghetti-like strands from squash. Add strands (about 3 cups) to pan; cook 2 minutes or until thoroughly heated.

7. Transfer to a bowl; add Parmesan cheese, sage, lemon rind, salt, and pepper, and toss well.

Know Your Ingredients

Garlic contains phytochemicals, compounds in plants that help protect people from infection and disease. Legend has it that ancient Egyptian soldiers ate garlic to give them more courage in battles.

Nutritional Information: Calories: 65 | Fat: 3 g | Saturated fat: 1.6 g | Monounsaturated fat: 0.03 g | Polyunsaturated fat: 0.17 g | Protein: 2 g | Carbohydrate: 10 g | Fiber: 2 g Cholesterol: 7 mg | Iron: 0.5 mg | Sodium: 285 mg | Calcium: 57 mg

CHAPTER 4

Ready for Dinner

Whether you call it dinner or supper, this is the last meal of the day—except for a possible bedtime snack! No matter how you label the meal, these recipes will help you end your day in an awesome way.

- Three-Bean Chunky Chili
- Spicy-Sweet Quesadilla Treats
- Guacamole Fish Tacos
- Fast and Delicious Sloppy-Joe Sliders

And many more yummy dishes!

SIMPLE

Pineapple-Bacon
Globe-Trotter Pizzas

Aloha! This is often called "Hawaiian" pizza, because so many pineapples are grown in Hawaii. It was invented by a Greek restaurant owner who lives in Canada. It's the most popular kind of pizza in Australia, so maybe it should be called the "G'day, mate" pizza. This pizza has been around the world!

Makes: 6 servings (serving size: 2 mini pizzas)

Ingredients
6 English muffins, split
1 (14-ounce) jar pizza sauce
1 (8-ounce) can pineapple tidbits in juice, drained
1 (6-ounce) package Canadian bacon, diced
1-1/2 cups shredded part-skim mozzarella cheese

Try This
For a no-chop pizza, use eight ounces of pepperoni in place of the bacon and pineapple.

Preparation
1. Preheat oven to 425°.

2. Spread pizza sauce evenly over the muffin halves, about 2 tablespoons of sauce for each.

3. Sprinkle pineapple and bacon evenly over the sauce. Then sprinkle cheese on top.

4. Place pizzas on a baking sheet. Bake for 12 minutes or until cheese is lightly browned.

Know Your Ingredients

Canadian bacon contains less fat than the popular bacon strips Americans often eat for breakfast.

Once canned pineapple is opened, refrigerate what's left in a sealed container and use within the week.

Fresh mozzarella can become watery when melted, so try to use regular mozzarella on pizza.

Nutritional Information: Calories: 273 | Fat: 7 g | Saturated fat: 3.5 g | Monounsaturated fat: 2.2 g | Polyunsaturated fat: 0.8 g | Protein: 17.3 g | Carbohydrate: 34.9 g | Fiber: 2.9 g | Cholesterol: 30 mg | Iron: 2.7 mg | Sodium: 867 mg | Calcium: 289 mg

Crushed and Crusty
Chips-and-Fish

Here's a delicious update on the classic fish-and-chips recipe. The tang in the salt-and-vinegar chips mellows as the fish bakes in the oven.

Makes: 4 fillets

Try This
Be environmentally friendly. Consider selecting cod that is caught by hook and line rather than by dragnets.

Feast on This
March 14 is National Potato Chip Day.

Ingredients

4 (6-ounce) cod fillets (or other firm whitefish)

2 teaspoons mayonnaise

1/8 teaspoon salt

1 (2-ounce) package salt-and-vinegar kettle-style potato chips, crushed

1/2 cup light ranch dressing

Preparation

1. Preheat oven to 400°. Arrange fillets on a parchment-lined baking sheet.

2. Brush mayonnaise evenly over top of fillets; sprinkle with salt.

3. Gently press crushed chips on tops of fillets, about 2 tablespoons per fillet.

4. Cook fish in oven for 10 minutes or until fish flakes easily when tested with a fork.

5. Serve with ranch dressing.

Riddle: What is a sea monster's favorite meal?
Answer: Fish-and-ships

Nutritional Information: Calories: 291 | Fat: 11.3 g | Saturated fat: 1.2 g | Monounsaturated fat: 5.7 g | Polyunsaturated fat: 2.8 g | Protein: 31.7 g | Carbohydrate: 14.5 g | Fiber: 0.8 g Cholesterol: 79 mg | Iron: 1.4 mg | Sodium: 549 mg | Calcium: 49 mg

Wheel in the Sky
Tortilla Pie

This one-pan chicken dinner takes its inspiration and ingredients from Mexico. Turn dinner into a fiesta!

Makes: 4 servings (serving size: 1 wedge)

Ingredients

2 cups cooked, shredded chicken breast
1/4 cup fresh salsa
1 cup black-bean dip (such as Guiltless Gourmet)
4 (8-inch) multigrain flour tortillas (such as Tumaro's)
1/2 cup (2 ounces) shredded reduced-fat Monterey Jack cheese
Cooking spray

Preparation

1. Preheat oven to 450°.

2. Combine chicken and salsa in a medium bowl.

3. Arrange tortillas across a work surface. Spread 1/4 cup black-bean dip over each tortilla.

4. Top tortillas evenly with chicken mixture and 2 tablespoons cheese.

5. Coat a 9-inch springform pan with cooking spray. Stack tortillas in bottom of pan.

6. Bake in oven for 10 minutes or until thoroughly heated and cheese melts.

7. Remove sides of pan. Cut pie into 4 wedges. Serve immediately.

Try This
Shred rotisserie chicken with the skin removed.

FROM

Many cultures prepare chicken in special ways. In the Philippines, chicken adobo is popular; it's marinated in vinegar and garlic. In India, tandoori chicken is prepared in a clay oven called a *tandoor*, then served with chutney, a spicy relish, and nann, a round, flat bread.

Nutritional Information: Calories: 380 | Fat: 11 g | Saturated fat: 4.3 g | Monounsaturated fat: 4.4 g | Polyunsaturated fat: 1.4 g | Protein: 39.9 g | Carbohydrate: 28.7 g | Fiber: 12.2 g Cholesterol: 80 mg | Iron: 0.8 mg | Sodium: 660 mg | Calcium: 215 mg

Three-Bean
Chunky Chili

Take this chili on camping trips or in a thermos for lunch.

Makes: 8 servings (serving size: 1 cup)

Know Your Ingredients

Pinto beans got their name from the Spanish word for "painted." They are smaller than kidney beans and are reddish brown and speckled. Both pinto and kidney beans are low in fat and are good sources of fiber.

Ingredients

1 tablespoon vegetable oil
2 cups chopped onions
1/2 cup chopped yellow bell pepper
1/2 cup chopped green bell pepper
2 garlic cloves, minced
1 tablespoon brown sugar
1-1/2 tablespoons chili powder
1 teaspoon ground cumin
1 teaspoon dried oregano
1/2 teaspoon salt
1/2 teaspoon black pepper
2 (16-ounce) cans stewed tomatoes, undrained
2 (15-ounce) cans black beans, rinsed and drained
1 (15-ounce) can kidney beans, rinsed and drained
1 (15-ounce) can pinto beans, rinsed and drained

Preparation

1. Heat the oil in a Dutch oven over medium-high heat.

2. Add onions, peppers, and garlic. Sauté 5 minutes or until tender.

3. Add sugar, chili powder, cumin, oregano, salt, pepper, tomatoes, and beans. Bring to a boil. Reduce heat, and simmer 30 minutes.

Feast on This

The annual International Chili Championship is held in Terlingua, Texas. Thousands of chili enthusiasts converge to cook their chili recipes in front of judges. For several days, RVs, tents, and booths create a sprawling community in this remote West Texas town near the Mexican border.

Terlingua

Try This

Just for fun, invent an all-red chili. Start with cooked kidney beans and add red onions, red peppers, red potatoes, and chopped tomatoes. Cook for an hour, and season with chili powder.

Nutritional Information: Calories: 257 | Fat: 2.7 g | Saturated fat: 0.3 g
Monounsaturated fat: 0.5 g | Polyunsaturated fat: 1.2 g | Protein: 12.8 g | Carbohydrate: 48.8 g
Fiber: 14.2 g | Cholesterol: 0 mg | Iron: 4.5 mg | Sodium: 876 mg | Calcium: 150 mg

'Wave It Up
Meat-Loaf Mugs

Various types of meat loaf are popular dishes around the world. Many cultures have their own combination of finely ground meats, bread crumbs, minced vegetables, and spices. These meat-loaf mugs bake up quickly thanks to the microwave oven.

Makes: 4 servings

Ingredients
1 pound extra-lean (92% lean) ground beef
1/2 cup quick-cooking oats
1 large egg
1 (5-1/2-ounce) can vegetable juice, such as V8
1/4 cup finely chopped green onions
1/4 cup finely chopped carrots
1/2 teaspoon salt
1/4 teaspoon pepper
1/4 cup ketchup

Preparation
1. Stir together beef, oats, egg, vegetable juice, onions, carrots, salt, and pepper in a big bowl.

2. Divide mixture evenly into four portions. Shape each portion into a ball. Place each ball into an 8-ounce microwave-safe coffee mug.

3. Line the bottom of the microwave with a sheet of waxed paper in case juices from the meat loaves bubble out. Place mugs in a circle on top of waxed paper. Cover mugs with another big sheet of waxed paper.

Feast on This
Rub your hands together quickly—you'll feel "friction heat." Microwave ovens work by causing this type of heat. Its pulsing, electromagnetic energy causes food's moisture molecules to rub against each other. This causes friction, which creates heat, and cooks your food.

4. Microwave for 11 minutes on medium-high (70% power). Check for doneness by cutting into meat loaves with a knife and fork. If any are still pink inside, microwave them for 30 seconds more and check again for doneness. Carefully remove each mug from the microwave using oven mitts.

5. Divide ketchup evenly on top of the meat loaves; cover with waxed paper, and let stand 2 minutes.

Be Safe
When cooking with a microwave oven, use dishes labeled 'microwave safe.' Heat food in glass containers rather than plastic, covered with paper towels to prevent splatters.

Nutritional Information: Calories: 246 | Fat: 11.1 g | Saturated fat: 4.6 g
Monounsaturated fat: 4.6 g | Polyunsaturated fat: 0.8 g | Protein: 25 g | Carbohydrate: 13.6 g
Fiber: 1.7 g | Cholesterol: 114 mg | Iron: 3.5 mg | Sodium: 653 mg | Calcium: 28 mg

Spicy-Sweet
Quesadilla Treats

MODERATE

A quesadilla relies on cheese as the "glue" to bind it with other ingredients. This recipe brings together chicken, sweet peaches, and spicy cheese.

Makes: 4 quesadillas

Ingredients
1 teaspoon honey
1/2 teaspoon fresh lime juice
1/2 cup reduced-fat sour cream
4 (8-inch) flour tortillas
3/4 cup (3 ounces) shredded Monterey Jack cheese
 with jalapeño peppers
1 cup chopped skinless, boneless rotisserie chicken breast
1 cup peeled, thinly sliced, firm, ripe peaches
4 teaspoons chopped fresh cilantro

Preparation

1. To make the sauce, combine honey and lime juice in a small bowl, stirring well with a whisk. Stir sour cream into honey mixture; cover and chill until ready to serve.

2. Place tortillas flat on a work surface. Sprinkle 3 tablespoons cheese over half of each tortilla; evenly divide chicken, peaches, and cilantro over cheese. Fold tortillas in half.

3. Heat a large nonstick skillet over medium-high heat. Coat pan with cooking spray.

Try This
For a milder version, use regular Monterey Jack or fontina cheese.

Know Your Ingredients
The peach, which originated in China, is a member of the rose family. It's a good source of vitamins A and C.

Nutritional Information: Calories: 364 | Fat: 15.8 g | Saturated fat: 7.4 g | Monounsaturated fat: 5.8 g | Polyunsaturated fat: 1.4 g | Protein: 21.3 g | Carbohydrate: 33.5 g | Fiber: 2.2 g Cholesterol: 68 mg | Iron: 2.1 mg | Sodium: 485 mg | Calcium: 235 mg

4. Place 2 quesadillas in the pan, and top quesadillas with a cast-iron or other heavy skillet.

5. Cook 1-1/2 minutes on each side or until tortillas are crisp and lightly browned (leave cast-iron skillet on quesadillas as they cook).

6. Remove quesadillas from pan; set aside, and keep warm.

7. Repeat steps 4 through 6.

8. Cut each quesadilla into wedges. Serve with the sauce.

Know Your Ingredients

Corn-tortilla quesadillas are preferred throughout Central and South America and most of Mexico. In northern Mexico and across the U.S., quesadillas are most commonly made with flour tortillas.

Home-Baked
Chicken Fingers

Here's a chicken-finger recipe you can make at home.

Makes: 5 servings (serving size: 3 chicken fingers)

Ingredients
2 tablespoons butter
1/3 cup all-purpose baking mix (such as Bisquick)
1/3 cup grated Parmesan cheese
1-1/2 teaspoons Old Bay seasoning
1/8 teaspoon black pepper
2 pounds boneless, skinless chicken-breast strips

Preparation

1. Preheat oven to 425°. Melt butter in a 10-by-15-inch jelly-roll pan in oven.

2. Place baking mix, cheese, seasoning, and pepper in a large zip-top plastic bag; shake well to combine.

3. Add chicken, several pieces at a time, shaking well to coat.

4. Arrange chicken in melted butter in jelly-roll pan.

5. Bake in oven for 30 minutes or until chicken is done, turning once. Serve immediately.

Try This
Freeze coated, uncooked chicken strips on a baking sheet. Then place them in a zip-top freezer bag and keep in the freezer until ready to use. Bake according to the recipe but with a slightly longer cooking time, turning after 25 minutes and baking for a total of 35 minutes.

80!

Nutritional Information: Calories: 294 | Fat: 8.7 g | Saturated fat: 4.5 g
Monounsaturated fat: 2.1 g | Polyunsaturated fat: 0.9 g | Protein: 44.7 g | Carbohydrate: 6 g
Fiber: 0 g | Cholesterol: 123 mg | Iron: 1.8 mg | Sodium: 516 mg | Calcium: 87 mg

MODERATE

Try This
Use packages of frozen baby-gold and white corn to capture freshness without the fuss of shucking ears or cutting kernels off the cob.

Corn and Bacon
Chowder Crocks

Early French immigrants to Canada made a hearty fish soup called *chaudree* (show-*dray*), named for the cauldron, or large pot, in which the soup was prepared. Further south, this soup came to be called "chowder," and its ingredients varied by region. In Maine, chowder included clams, potatoes, and water. In Massachusetts, cooks added milk. In Connecticut and Manhattan, they added tomato.

Makes: 6 servings (serving size: 1 cup)

Ingredients
2 bacon slices
1/2 cup refrigerated chopped celery, onion, and bell-pepper mix
2 (16-ounce) packages frozen baby-gold and white corn, thawed and divided
2 cups 1% low-fat milk
1/2 teaspoon salt
1/4 teaspoon freshly ground black pepper
3/4 cup (3 ounces) shredded reduced-fat extra-sharp cheddar cheese (such as Cracker Barrel)
Freshly ground black pepper (optional)

Preparation
1. Cook bacon in a Dutch oven over medium heat until crisp. Remove bacon from pan; crumble and set aside.

2. Add celery mixture and 1 package of corn to drippings in pan. Sauté 5 minutes or until vegetables are tender.

3. Place remaining package of corn and 1 cup of milk in a blender, and process until smooth.

4. Add pureed mixture to vegetables in pan. Stir in the remaining milk and the salt, pepper, and cheese. Cook over medium heat (do not boil), stirring constantly, until cheese melts.

5. Use a soup ladle to put chowder into bowls. Top servings evenly with crumbled bacon. Sprinkle with additional black pepper, if desired.

Other hearty foods enjoyed by Canadians include *poutine* (poo-*teen*), which is made with layers of french fries smothered in cheese curds and beef gravy, and *tourtière* (tor-tee-*air*), a traditional holiday meat-pie cooked with herbs and gravy.

U.S. Crops
The U.S. is the world's largest exporter of corn. Here are the country's top crop exports:

1. Corn
2. Soybeans
3. Wheat
4. Sugar beets
5. Sugar cane

Source: Food and Agriculture Organization of the United Nations, Agricultural Production data, 2010

Nutritional Information: Calories: 215 | Fat: 6 g | Saturated fat: 3.1 g
Monounsaturated fat: 1 g | Polyunsaturated fat: 0.6 g | Protein: 10.8 g | Carbohydrate: 33.6 g
Fiber: 3.8 g | Cholesterol: 15 mg | Iron: 0.8 mg | Sodium: 402 mg | Calcium: 208 mg

Guacamole
Fish Tacos

Brighten up weeknight dinners with these easy and flavorful tacos. The guacamole is very creamy and tasty on its own, so make extra if you'd like.

Makes: 4 servings (serving size: 2 tacos)

Ingredients
1/2 cup thinly sliced red onion
1 tablespoon fresh lime juice
3/4 teaspoon kosher salt
2 ripe avocados, peeled and mashed
Cooking spray
2 (10-ounce) yellowfin tuna steaks
   (about 1 inch thick)
8 (6-inch) corn tortillas

Preparation
1. Combine the onion, lime juice, 1/4 teaspoon salt, and avocados.

2. Heat a grill pan over medium-high heat; coat pan with cooking spray.

3. Sprinkle tuna with remaining 1/2 teaspoon salt.

4. Add tuna to pan; cook 4 minutes on each side or to desired degree of doneness. Cut tuna into 1/4-inch-thick slices.

5. Warm tortillas according to the package directions. Divide avocado mixture evenly among tortillas. Divide tuna evenly among tortillas.

Feast on This

Mexico is the world's top producer of avocados, with California coming in second. Florida is the second-biggest producer in the United States.

An average of 53.5 million pounds of guacamole are eaten in the U.S. every Super Bowl Sunday, enough to cover a football field more than 20 feet deep.

Know Your Ingredients

Yellowfin tuna can grow to 400 pounds, and can live to about seven years. They are near the top of the food chain, feeding on fish, squid, and crustaceans. They are prey for top predators such as sharks—and humans.

Nutritional Information: Calories: 402 | Fat: 17.3 g | Saturated fat: 2.5 g | Monounsaturated fat: 10.1 g | Polyunsaturated fat: 2.7 g | Protein: 37.3 g | Carbohydrate: 28.2 g | Fiber: 9 g
Cholesterol: 64 mg | Iron: 1.6 mg | Sodium: 430 mg | Calcium: 59 mg

Grilled Chicken
Super Kebabs

Roasted or grilled meats are eaten hundreds of different ways in the Middle East. One popular style is the shish kebab, small chunks of meat cooked on a skewer. For this recipe, you will need 16 six-inch metal skewers. Remember to keep sharp skewer tips away from little brothers and sisters!

Makes: 4 servings (serving size: 2 kebabs)

Try This
For an easy side dish, toss one head of Bibb lettuce with 1/2 cup drained mandarin oranges. Serve with ginger salad dressing from the grocery store.

Ingredients
Olive Oil Marinade

1/3 cup red-wine vinegar
1/3 cup olive oil
4 garlic cloves, pressed
1 tablespoon fresh rosemary leaves
1 teaspoon salt
1 teaspoon Dijon mustard

Chicken and Vegetables

1 pound skinned and boned chicken breasts, cut into
  2-inch pieces
1 large green bell pepper, cut into 2-inch pieces
1 pint cherry tomatoes
1 (8-ounce) package fresh mushrooms
16 (6-inch) metal skewers

Preparation
Part One: Olive Oil Marinade

1. Preheat grill to about 350° or 400° (medium-high heat).

2. In a small bowl, whisk together vinegar, oil, garlic, rosemary, salt, and mustard.

Part Two: Chicken and Vegetables

1. Pour half of olive oil marinade into a shallow bowl or zip-top plastic freezer bag. Add chicken, turning to coat. Cover or seal, and let stand 10 minutes.

2. Pour remaining marinade into another bowl or freezer bag; add bell pepper, tomatoes, and mushrooms, and toss to coat. Cover or seal, and let stand 10 minutes.

3. Remove chicken and vegetables from marinade, discarding marinade.

Part Three: Kebab Preparation

1. Thread chicken onto 8 skewers. Thread vegetables alternately onto the other 8 skewers.

2. Grill kebabs, covered with grill lid, 10 to 12 minutes or until chicken is done and vegetables are tender, turning occasionally.

3. Remove kebabs from grill. Let stand 5 minutes before serving.

Nutritional Information: Calories: 334
Fat: 21 g | Saturated fat: 3 g
Monounsaturated fat: 14 g
Polyunsaturated fat: 3 g | Protein: 29 g
Carbohydrate: 9 g | Fiber: 2 g
Cholesterol: 66 mg | Iron: 2 mg
Sodium: 704 mg | Calcium: 33 mg

Chicken Drumette
Dipping Wings

The drumette is the fleshier half of the chicken wing; it looks like a little drumstick.

Makes: 12 servings (serving size: 3 drumettes)

Ingredients
1 tablespoon dried thyme
1 tablespoon dried oregano
1 tablespoon ground cumin
1 tablespoon paprika
1 teaspoon onion powder
1 teaspoon salt
1/2 teaspoon pepper
5 pounds chicken drumettes
Garnish: green-onion curls (see sidebar)
White Barbecue Sauce (see page 117)

Preparation
Part One: Herbs Mixture

1. In a small bowl, combine thyme, oregano, cumin, paprika, onion powder, salt, and pepper.

2. Rinse chicken, and pat dry. Rub herb mixture over chicken.

3. Place chicken in a zip-top plastic freezer bag. Seal bag, and chill 4 to 24 hours.

4. Remove chicken from bag, then discard bag.

Part Two: Grilled Chicken

1. Preheat grill to 350° to 400° (medium-high heat).

Try This
To curl green onions, have an adult run a sharp knife's tip down the middle of the onion, from the white end to the green end. Turn the onion and make two more lengthwise slices the same way. Then drop onion strips into cold water.

2. Grill chicken, covered with grill lid, 20 to 25 minutes or until done, turning once.

3. Garnish, if desired. Serve with White Barbecue Sauce.

Nutritional Information:
Calories: 415 | Fat: 33 g
Saturated fat: 6 g
Monounsaturated fat: 9.5 g
Polyunsaturated fat: 13 g
Protein: 25 g | Carbohydrate: 2 g
Fiber: 1 g | Cholesterol: 113 mg
Iron: 2 mg | Sodium: 695 mg
Calcium: 32 mg

White Barbecue Sauce
Ingredients
1-1/2 cups mayonnaise
1/4 cup white-wine vinegar
1 garlic clove, minced
1 tablespoon coarsely ground pepper
1 tablespoon spicy brown mustard
1 teaspoon sugar
1 teaspoon salt
2 teaspoons horseradish

Preparation
1. Stir together mayonnaise, vinegar, garlic, pepper, mustard, sugar, salt, and horseradish until well blended.

2. Store in an airtight container in refrigerator for up to 1 week.

Nutritional Information: Calories: 88 | Fat: 9 g | Saturated fat: 1 g | Monounsaturated fat: 2.5 g | Polyunsaturated fat: 5 g | Protein: 0 g | Carbohydrate: 0.5 g | Fiber: 0 g Cholesterol: 4 mg | Iron: 0 mg | Sodium: 168 mg | Calcium: 1 mg

Know Your Ingredients
Mushrooms, onions, cauliflower, and turnips are examples of white foods with disease-fighting phytochemicals. Garlic and ginger are also full of health-promoting substances.

MODERATE

Special Pork
Posole Soup

Posole (po-*soh*-lay) is a thick and chunky soup that is native to Mexico. In Mexico, it is so popular that restaurants called *pozolerías* cater to its many fans. *Posole* means "foamy": Boiling the pork creates a layer of foam on top of the soup.

Makes: 4 servings (serving size: 1–1/3 cups)

Ingredients
Cooking spray
1 (1-pound) pork tenderloin, trimmed and cut into
    bite-size pieces
2 teaspoons salt-free Southwest seasoning blend
1 (15-1/2-ounce) can white hominy, undrained
1 (14-1/2-ounce) can Mexican-style stewed tomatoes, undrained
1 cup water
1/4 cup chopped fresh cilantro

Preparation
1. Heat a large saucepan over medium-high heat. Coat pan with cooking spray.

2. Sprinkle pork evenly with Southwest seasoning blend.

3. Add pork to pan; cook 2 minutes each side or until browned.

4. Stir in hominy, tomatoes, and water. Bring to a boil. Cover, reduce heat, and simmer 20 minutes or until pork is tender. Stir in cilantro.

Try This
Let the pork cook until it no longer sticks to the pan.

Serve posole with warm tortillas and garnishes like shredded cabbage, chopped onion, oregano, limes, hard rolls, and red chilies.

Feast on This

The first written mention of posole was in the 1500s, by Spanish explorers traveling through what is now Mexico.

Nutritional Information: Calories: 233 | Fat: 5 g | Saturated fat: 1.4 g | Monounsaturated fat: 1.9 g | Polyunsaturated fat: 0.8 g | Protein: 24.4 g | Carbohydrate: 23 g
Fiber: 4.4 g | Cholesterol: 68 mg | Iron: 2.3 mg | Sodium: 610 mg | Calcium: 33 mg

Have It Your Way
Veggie Burgers

These delicious no-meat burgers are great for a weekend meal, either indoors or out.

Makes: 6 burgers

Ingredients
1 (15-ounce) can chickpeas (garbanzo beans), rinsed
    and drained
1 cup sliced green onions
2/3 cup freshly grated Parmesan cheese
1/2 teaspoon salt
1 (8-ounce) can cut green beans, drained
1 tablespoon lemon-pepper seasoning
1 garlic clove, minced
1 cup cooked brown rice
Cooking spray
6 whole wheat hamburger buns
Condiments: ketchup, mustard, pickles, onion slices, tomato slices, lettuce, alfalfa sprouts (optional)

Preparation
1. Combine chickpeas, green onions, cheese, salt, green beans, lemon-pepper seasoning, and garlic in a food-processor bowl. Pulse 3 to 4 times or until chopped.

2. Transfer mixture to a large bowl, and stir in rice. Cover and chill mixture at least 1 hour.

3. Shape vegetable mixture into 6 bun-size patties.

4. Heat a large nonstick skillet over medium heat until hot. Coat patties with cooking spray.

Feast on This
India grows the most garbanzo beans, also called chickpeas, in the world. Chickpeas are very popular in Indian cuisine. They are ground up to make flour, eaten in salads and stews, and fried as falafel.

5. Cook patties (in batches if necessary), in skillet over medium heat, 6 minutes on each side or until browned.

6. Transfer patties to a plate, and let cool slightly. Serve patties on whole wheat buns with condiments.

Nutritional Information: Calories: 263 | Fat: 7 g | Saturated fat: 2.2 g | Monounsaturated fat: 1.6 g | Polyunsaturated fat: 1.5 g | Protein: 12.5 g | Carbohydrate: 40 g | Fiber: 6.5 g | Cholesterol: 9 mg | Iron: 2 mg | Sodium: 893 mg | Calcium: 256 mg

Shrimp "Fried"
Confetti Rice

Fried rice is an ancient specialty from the Chinese city of Yangzhou. It is made with leftovers and cooked in woks. Check out this alternative to the one on the Chinese take-out menu.

wok a metal pan with a curved bottom; it is used to cook Chinese cuisine

Makes: 6 servings (serving size: about 1–1/3 cups)

Ingredients
3 (3-1/2-ounce) bags boil-in-bag brown rice
Cooking spray
2 large eggs, lightly beaten
1 tablespoon canola oil
12 ounces medium shrimp, peeled and deveined
3 tablespoons lower-sodium soy sauce
2 tablespoons rice vinegar
1 teaspoon dark sesame oil
1/4 teaspoon salt
1 cup chopped green onions
1 tablespoon minced fresh ginger
2 cups frozen petite green peas

**Feast
on This**
Fried rice contains high amounts of carbohydrates, an important energy source—the brain uses only carbohydrates for energy. And the protein in fried rice is important for keeping your body in excellent shape.

Preparation
1. Cook rice according to package directions, omitting salt and fat; drain. Remove rice from bags; return to pan. Cover and keep warm.

2. While rice cooks, heat a large nonstick skillet over medium-high heat. Coat pan with cooking spray.

3. Add eggs to pan; cook 1 minute or until set. Remove eggs from pan; coarsely chop.

4. Return pan to heat; add oil. Add shrimp; cook 2 minutes, stirring often.

Try This
Chewing a piece of
ginger or ginger candy
may help relieve an
upset stomach.

5. While shrimp cooks, combine soy sauce, rice vinegar, sesame oil, and salt in a small bowl.

6. Add onions and ginger to shrimp; sauté 1 minute.

7. Add peas, stirring until thoroughly heated.

8. Stir shrimp mixture and egg into rice, and drizzle with soy-sauce mixture. Fluff well with a fork, and serve immediately.

Nutritional Information: Calories: 335 | Fat: 7.2 g | Saturated fat: 1 g | Monounsaturated fat: 2.6 g | Polyunsaturated fat: 1.7 g | Protein: 21.1 g | Carbohydrate: 46.9 g | Fiber: 5 g Cholesterol: 157 mg | Iron: 3.4 mg | Sodium: 583 mg | Calcium: 85 mg

On Top of Old Smoky
Spaghetti with Meatballs

Before coming to the United States in the mid-1800s, Italians ate meat only a few times a month. When they arrived, meat was so plentiful, they incorporated more of it into their cooking. Meatballs are an Italian-American invention.

Makes: 4 servings (serving size: about 1–1/4 cups)

Ingredients
1 (9-ounce) package refrigerated fettuccine
1 (12-ounce) package bulk sweet Italian turkey-sausage meat
1 tablespoon extra-virgin olive oil
2 cups sliced onions
1/4 teaspoon crushed red pepper flakes
2 large garlic cloves, crushed
2 cups lower-sodium marinara sauce (such as McCutcheon's)
1/2 ounce pecorino cheese, grated (about 2 tablespoons packed)
8 fresh basil leaves, torn

Preparation
1. Cook the pasta according to package directions, omitting salt and fat; drain.

2. Shape sausage into 12 (1-inch) balls.

3. Heat a large skillet over medium-high heat. Add oil to pan; swirl to coat.

4. Add meatballs to pan; cook 7 minutes, browning on all sides. Remove the meatballs from pan.

5. Add onions, red pepper, and garlic to pan; sauté for 2 minutes. Return meatballs and add marinara sauce to pan, and bring to a simmer over medium heat, scraping pan to loosen browned bits.

Try This
Why not grow simple cooking herbs indoors? Basil, dill, chives, fennel, sage, thyme, lavender, mint, parsley, rosemary, and oregano can be grown in a sunny area of your home.

6. Reduce heat to medium-low, and simmer 5 minutes or until meatballs are done.

7. Add cooked pasta to sauce mixture; toss well. Sprinkle with cheese and fresh basil.

Feast on This

The average person in North America eats about 15-1/2 pounds of pasta per year. The average person in Italy eats more than 51 pounds of pasta every year.

Source: National Pasta Association

Nutritional Information: Calories: 412 | Fat: 14 g | Saturated fat: 4.2 g | Monounsaturated fat: 5.4 g | Polyunsaturated fat: 3.1 g | Protein: 19.2 g | Carbohydrate: 77.7 g | Fiber: 2.6 g Cholesterol: 77 mg | Iron: 2.6 mg | Sodium: 632 mg | Calcium: 43 mg

Fast and Delicious
Sloppy-Joe Sliders

The name "slider" may have originated in the galley kitchens of U.S. naval ships, where hamburgers would slide across the griddle as the ship rocked in heavy seas. It may also refer to the ease with which these tiny tempters slide down your throat in one or two bites.

Feast on This
Sloppy Joes are "loose meat" sandwiches thought to be named for a cook who invented them in 1930. They're also called "wimpies," "yip yips," and "slushburgers."

Makes: 4 servings (serving size: 2 sliders)

Ingredients
Slider

1/2 cup julienne-cut carrots
10 ounces lean ground beef
3/4 cup chopped onion
1 teaspoon garlic powder
1 teaspoon chili powder
1/4 teaspoon freshly ground black pepper
8 slider hamburger buns

Ketchup Mixture

1/4 cup ketchup
1 tablespoon Dijon mustard
1 tablespoon Worcestershire sauce
1 tablespoon tomato paste
1 teaspoon red-wine vinegar
1 (8-ounce) can no-salt-added tomato sauce

Preparation
Part One: **Slider**

1. Preheat broiler.

2. Heat a large nonstick skillet over medium-high heat.

3. Add carrots, beef, and onion to pan; cook 6 minutes or until beef is browned and vegetables are tender.

4. Add garlic powder, chili powder, and pepper; cook 1 minute.

Part Two:
Ketchup Mixture

1. In a small bowl, combine ketchup, mustard, Worcestershire sauce, tomato paste, vinegar, and tomato sauce.

2. Add ketchup mixture to pan, stirring to evenly coat beef mixture. Simmer for 5 minutes or until thickened.

Part Three:
Slider Assembly

1. While sauce thickens, arrange buns, cut side up, in a single layer on a baking sheet. Broil 2 minutes or until lightly toasted.

2. Place about 1/2 cup beef mixture in each bun.

Nutritional Information: Calories: 373 | Fat: 10 g | Saturated fat: 3.6g | Monounsaturated fat: 3.5 g | Polyunsaturated fat: 2.3 g | Protein: 23.1 g | Carbohydrate: 52.2 g | Fiber: 4.2 g Cholesterol: 38 mg | Iron: 4 mg | Sodium: 736 mg | Calcium: 111 mg

Nature's Nectar
Glazed Salmon

Impress your family by making tangy sautéed salmon. Salmon contains omega-3 fats, which are good for your heart and boost your brain power.

Makes: 4 fillets

Ingredients

2 tablespoons fresh lemon juice
2 tablespoons maple syrup
1 tablespoon cider vinegar
1 tablespoon canola oil
4 (6-ounce) skinless salmon fillets
1/2 teaspoon salt
1/4 teaspoon freshly ground black pepper
Cooking spray

Preparation

1. Combine lemon juice, maple syrup, vinegar, and oil in a large zip-top plastic bag. Add fish to bag; seal. Refrigerate 10 minutes, turning bag once.

2. Preheat broiler.

3. Remove fish from bag, reserving marinade. Place marinade in a microwave-safe bowl. Microwave on high for 1 minute.

4. Heat a large ovenproof nonstick skillet over medium-high heat.

5. Sprinkle fish evenly with salt and pepper. Coat pan with cooking spray. Add fish to pan; cook 3 minutes. Turn fish over. Brush marinade evenly over fish.

6. Broil 3 minutes or until fish flakes easily when tested with a fork or until it reaches desired degree of doneness.

Know Your Ingredients

Many salmon are anadromous (an-*ad*-ro-mus), which means they spend most of their lives in the ocean but return to freshwater—in the river where they were born—to spawn.

Try This

Finish the fish under the broiler to caramelize the glaze into a tasty browned crust. Serve with roasted potato wedges and peas.

FROM

TIME
FOR KIDS

Wild salmon get a lot more exercise than farm-raised salmon, making them much leaner, with a higher proportion of protein and less fat.

Nutritional Information: Calories: 287 | Fat: 14 g | Saturated fat: 2.7 g
Monounsaturated fat: 6.7 g | Polyunsaturated fat: 3.6 g | Protein: 31 g | Carbohydrate: 7.5 g
Fiber: 0.1 g | Cholesterol: 80 mg | Iron: 0.7 mg | Sodium: 363 mg | Calcium: 23 mg

CHAPTER 5

What's for Dessert?

Once upon a time, dessert was an end-of-the-day treat eaten by wealthy people. Fortunately, life has become sweeter over the years and today, dessert is enjoyed by everybody. Eaten in moderation, the treats in this chapter are a wonderful way to end a meal. And when they include healthful ingredients like dark chocolate, a power food, desserts help you score a health home run.

● Gingersnap Chilly Willies

● Easy & Perfect Vanilla Pudding

● Here Comes Simon the Centipede!

● Big 'n' Crunchy Sugar Cookies

   And many more yummy treats!

MODERATE

Gingersnap
Chilly Willies

The forecast calls for a cold (ginger) snap! You'll be one cool cookie serving these ice cream sandwiches with their unique combination of flavors.

Makes: **8 ice cream sandwiches**

Ingredients

3 tablespoons no-sugar-added creamy peanut butter
2 cups no-sugar-added, fat-free vanilla ice cream, softened
16 (2-inch-diameter) gingersnap cookies

Preparation

1. Swirl peanut butter into ice cream. Place in freezer 30 minutes or until firm enough to spread.

2. Divide ice cream mixture evenly onto 8 gingersnap cookies. Top with remaining cookies.

3. Place sandwiches on a 15-by-10-inch jelly-roll pan; freeze until firm.

4. Wrap each sandwich in plastic wrap, and store in freezer.

Know Your Ingredients

The spice ginger, which is found in gingersnap cookies, comes from ginger root. First grown in Southeast Asia, it is still prized for its positive effects on health.

Nutritional Information: Calories: 124 | Fat: 4.7 g | Saturated fat: 0.9 g
Monounsaturated fat: 0 g | Polyunsaturated fat: 0 g | Protein: 4.3 g | Carbohydrate: 18.1 g
Fiber: 0.9 g | Cholesterol: 4 mg | Iron: 0 mg | Sodium: 52 mg | Calcium: 0 mg

Melt in Your Mouth
Chocolate Cupcakes

These cupcakes are perfect for chocolate lovers.

Makes: 2 dozen cupcakes

Ingredients

1 (18.25-ounce) package German chocolate cake mix
1 (16-ounce) container sour cream
1/4 cup butter, melted
2 large eggs
1 teaspoon vanilla extract
Cooking spray
Chocolate Buttercream Frosting (see page 135)
Thin mints, shaved with a vegetable peeler for garnish (optional)

Preparation

1. Preheat oven to 350°.

2. Beat cake mix, sour cream, butter, eggs, and vanilla at low speed with an electric mixer just until dry ingredients are moistened.

3. Increase speed to medium, and beat 3 to 4 minutes or until smooth, stopping to scrape bowl as needed.

4. Place paper baking cups in muffin pans, and coat with cooking spray. Spoon batter evenly into baking cups, filling each cup two-thirds full.

5. Bake in preheated oven for 25 minutes or until a wooden toothpick inserted in center comes out clean.

6. Cool in pans on wire racks 10 minutes. Then place cupcakes directly on wire racks, and cool 1 hour or until completely cool.

7. Spread Chocolate Buttercream Frosting on the cupcakes.

Nutritional Information: Calories: 148 | Fat: 7.5 g | Saturated fat: 4 g
Monounsaturated fat: 1.5 g | Polyunsaturated fat: 0.5 g | Protein: 2 g | Carbohydrate: 18 g
Fiber: 1 g | Cholesterol: 35 mg | Iron: 0.5 mg | Sodium: 164 mg | Calcium: 36 mg

Chocolate Buttercream Frosting

Ingredients

1/2 cup butter, softened
1 teaspoon vanilla extract
1/8 teaspoon salt
1 (16-ounce) package powdered sugar
2/3 cup unsweetened cocoa
5 to 7 tablespoons milk

Preparation

1. Beat butter, vanilla, and salt at medium speed with an electric mixer until creamy.

2. In a separate bowl, whisk together powdered sugar and cocoa.

3. Gradually add the sugar mixture and milk to the butter mixture, alternating between the sugar and 1 tablespoon milk at a time, up to 5 tablespoons milk. Beat at low speed until blended and smooth after each addition. (If needed, slowly beat in up to 2 tablespoons more milk.)

Nutritional Information: Calories: 79 | Fat: 4 g | Saturated fat: 2 g | Monounsaturated fat: 0.6 g | Polyunsaturated fat: 0.1 g | Protein: 0 g | Carbohydrate: 12 g | Fiber: 0 g
Cholesterol: 8 mg | Iron: 0 mg | Sodium: 20 mg | Calcium: 4 mg

Feast on This

Cooks around the world are inventing new kinds of cupcakes. Imagine trying flavors like dark chocolate and avocado, or bacon and maple syrup! One cook entered Britain's National Cupcake Championships with the smallest cupcake ever: It was just over a half inch tall by one inch wide.

Easy & Perfect
Vanilla Pudding

You'll probably have all the ingredients for this pudding recipe without even going to the store. And check out the decorating choices.

Makes: **4 servings (serving size: 1/2 cup)**

Ingredients
1/4 cup sugar
2 tablespoons cornstarch
1/8 teaspoon salt
2 cups milk
1 teaspoon vanilla extract
Whipped topping (optional)
Candy sprinkles (optional)

Preparation

1. Combine sugar, cornstarch, and salt in a medium saucepan. Whisk in milk.

2. Bring to a boil over medium heat, whisking constantly. Cook, stirring constantly, 1 minute or until pudding thickens. Remove from heat, and stir in vanilla.

3. Pour pudding into a small bowl. Cool to room temperature, stirring occasionally.

4. Cover with plastic wrap, and chill in the refrigerator at least 3 hours.

5. Serve pudding with whipped topping and sprinkles, if you'd like, or decorate as in the Puddin' Heads recipe below.

Nutritional Information: Calories: 140 | Fat: 4 g | Saturated fat: 2.3 g
Monounsaturated fat: 1 g | Polyunsaturated fat: 0.2 g | Protein: 3.9 g
Carbohydrate: 21.8 g | Fiber: 0 g | Cholesterol: 12 mg | Iron: 0.1 mg | Sodium: 122 mg
Calcium: 138 mg

Know Your Ingredients

When vanilla beans are harvested, they still do not have their distinctive fragrance and flavor. The beans develop these properties during the drying process.

Puddin' Heads
Ingredients

Easy & Perfect Vanilla Pudding (see page 136)
Cereal, grapes, blueberries, orange slices, strawberries, kiwi, gumdrops

Preparation

1. Spoon pudding into serving bowls.

2. Use chopped fruits and other suggested decorations to create fun faces.

Nutritional Information: Calories: 143 | Fat: 4 g | Saturated fat: 2.3 g
Monounsaturated fat: 1 g | Polyunsaturated fat: 0.2 g | Protein: 4 g
Carbohydrate: 22.7 g | Fiber: 0.2 g | Cholesterol: 12 mg | Iron: 0.1 mg
Sodium: 122 mg | Calcium: 140 mg

1, 2, 3—Freeze!
Chocolate Ice Cream

When it's hot outside, chill out. Make ice cream by freezing three kinds of milk three times! It's guaranteed to cool you down on a summer day.

Makes: **1–1/4 quarts (serving size: about 2/3 cup)**

Ingredients

1 (14-ounce) can sweetened condensed milk
1 (5-ounce) can evaporated milk
2 cups whole chocolate milk
2/3 cup chocolate syrup
3/4 cup toasted, sliced almonds

Preparation

1. Whisk the condensed, evaporated, and chocolate milks with chocolate syrup in a 2-quart pitcher or large bowl until blended. Cover and chill in the freezer for 30 minutes.

2. Pour milk mixture into the freezer container of a 1-quart electric ice-cream maker. Freeze in the ice-cream maker according to manufacturer's instructions. (Instructions and times will vary.)

3. Remove the container with ice cream from the ice-cream maker, and place it in your freezer for 15 minutes.

4. Stir almonds into the prepared ice cream, then scoop ice cream into an airtight container. Freeze again until firm, or about 1 to 1-1/2 hours.

Feast on This

The average number of licks to polish off a single-scoop ice-cream cone is approximately 50.

More ice cream is sold on Sunday than any other day of the week.

Feast on This

"Brain freeze," a brief headache, is triggered when ice cream touches the roof of your mouth, causing blood vessels in the head to dilate. If you press your tongue on the roof of your mouth, the brain freeze will go away.

Nutritional Information: Calories: 350 | Fat: 12 g | Saturated fat: 5 g
Monounsaturated fat: 5 g | Polyunsaturated fat: 1.3 g | Protein: 9.5 g | Carbohydrate: 53 g
Fiber: 1.5 g | Cholesterol: 30 mg | Iron: 1 mg | Sodium: 134 mg | Calcium: 278 mg

Creamy Berry
Fruit Pops

These delicious freezer pops are made with fresh, natural ingredients, including honey, which is very good for you!

Makes: **10 pops (serving size: 1 pop)**

Know Your Ingredients
Choose all-natural foods instead of processed foods whenever possible.

Ingredients
1 cup low-fat vanilla yogurt
1 banana
3 cups fresh or frozen raspberries
1/2 cup honey
Craft sticks
10 (2-ounce) pop molds

Preparation
1. In a blender, process yogurt and banana for 30 seconds or until smooth.

2. In a medium saucepan, bring raspberries and honey to a boil over medium-high heat. Reduce heat to low, and simmer 5 minutes.

3. Pour raspberry mixture through a fine wire-mesh strainer into a bowl, using back of spoon to squeeze out juice and pulp. Throw away skins and seeds.

4. Cover and chill raspberry mixture 30 minutes.

5. Pour yogurt mixture evenly into pop molds.

6. Top with raspberry mixture, and swirl, if desired.

7. Top with lid of pop mold, and insert craft sticks, leaving 1-1/2 to 2 inches sticking out of pop.

8. Freeze for 6 hours or until sticks are solidly anchored and pops are completely frozen.

FROM
TIME
FOR KIDS

Food companies add sugar to many items, from ketchup to crackers. There are pasta sauces with more added sugar than in ice-cream toppings. The typical kid eats the equivalent of 20 teaspoons of sugar every day.

Try This
Substitute blueberries or halved strawberries for raspberries.

Nutritional Information: Calories: 105 | Fat: 0.5 g | Saturated fat: 0.16 g
Monounsaturated fat: 0.1 g | Polyunsaturated fat: 0.14 g | Protein: 1 g | Carbohydrate: 26 g
Fiber: 3 g | Cholesterol: 1.5 mg | Iron: 0 mg | Sodium: 16 mg | Calcium: 40 mg

All-Time Favorite
Choc Chip Cookies

Chocolate has been scientifically proven to allow happiness to, well, happen. Eating chocolate has been linked to the release of endorphins and serotonin, brain fuels that help people relax and keep calm.

Makes: 60 cookies (serving size: 1 cookie)

Feast on This

A 12,000-pound chocolate bar made with 1,200 pounds of almonds, 5,500 pounds of sugar, and 1,700 pounds of cocoa butter toured U.S. schools. The reason: To help teach students to "think big" by practicing portion control and moderation in eating.

Ingredients

3/4 cup butter, softened
3/4 cup granulated sugar
3/4 cup firmly packed dark brown sugar
2 large eggs
1-1/2 teaspoons vanilla extract
2-1/4 cups plus 2 tablespoons all-purpose flour
1 teaspoon baking soda
3/4 teaspoon salt
1-1/2 (12-ounce) packages semisweet chocolate morsels
Parchment paper

Preparation

1. Preheat oven to 350°. Beat butter and sugars with a mixer at medium speed until creamy. Add eggs and vanilla, beating until blended.

2. Combine flour, baking soda, and salt in a small bowl. Gradually add to butter mixture, beating just until blended. Beat in chocolate morsels just until combined.

3. Line baking sheets with parchment paper. Drop cookie dough by tablespoonfuls onto baking sheets.

4. Bake in preheated oven for 10 to 14 minutes or until desired degree of doneness. Remove to wire racks, and cool completely (about 15 minutes).

Feast on This

Fine, dark chocolate is made from ground cacao beans. Filled with many beneficial nutrients, dark chocolate has been shown to have a positive effect on our blood pressure, cardiovascular system, circulation, and overall energy.

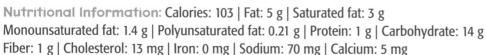

Nutritional Information: Calories: 103 | Fat: 5 g | Saturated fat: 3 g
Monounsaturated fat: 1.4 g | Polyunsaturated fat: 0.21 g | Protein: 1 g | Carbohydrate: 14 g
Fiber: 1 g | Cholesterol: 13 mg | Iron: 0 mg | Sodium: 70 mg | Calcium: 5 mg

Here Comes
Simon the Centipede!

Make this for a special birthday party or for some family fun.

Makes: **6 centipedes (serving size: 1 centipede)**

Feast on This

More than 362 billion Oreo cookies have been sold since they were first introduced in 1912. In the U.S., Oreos are baked in a 300-foot oven—that's about the length of a football field!

Ingredients

1 (8-ounce) container frozen whipped topping, thawed
1/2 to 1 teaspoon green liquid food coloring
36 vanilla wafers
1 or 2 bananas, peeled and cut to make a total of 36 slices
Miniature candy-coated chocolate pieces
1 cherry-flavored chewy fruit roll
6 uncooked spaghetti strands
Pull-and-peel red candy ropes
Crumbled Oreos (optional)

Preparation

Part One: Body

1. Place whipped topping in a medium bowl. Gently fold in food coloring.

2. Spread 1 teaspoon whipped topping on the flat side of 1 vanilla wafer. Top with 1 banana slice. Repeat for all wafers.

3. Carefully stand 6 wafer/banana stacks on their edges, one after another, in a slightly curved line. Repeat to make 6 centipedes.

4. Spread remaining whipped topping on bodies, covering completely. Cover and chill in the refrigerator at least 8 hours.

Part Two: Eyes, Spots, and Mouth

1. Attach chocolate pieces to centipedes to make eyes and spots. Cut fruit roll into small pieces, and attach to make a mouth for each centipede.

Part Three:
Antennas and Legs

1. Snap spaghetti strands in half. Separate candy ropes into strands. Cut candy strands into 12 (7-inch) segments.

2. Tie a loose knot close to end of 1 candy strand. Insert tip of 1 strand of spaghetti into knot, and carefully tighten. Starting at knot, wind candy strand around the spaghetti, pressing gently as you go so the candy sticks to the spaghetti. Break the spaghetti off about an inch below the strand.

3. Repeat the process with remaining candy strands around spaghetti strands. Insert 2 spaghetti/candy "antennas" into each centipede, just above the eyes.

4. Separate more candy ropes into thin strands. Make Simon's legs by cutting candy strands into 72 (1-inch) segments, then stick them into the sides of each centipede, 6 legs on each side. Optional: Serve each centipede on a bed of crumbled-Oreo "soil."

Nutritional Information: Calories: 282 | Fat: 13 g | Saturated fat: 6.6 g
Monounsaturated fat: 0 g | Polyunsaturated fat: 0 g | Protein: 2.6 g | Carbohydrate: 36.3 g
Fiber: 0.5 g | Cholesterol: 6 mg | Iron: 1.4 mg | Sodium: 156 mg | Calcium: 1 mg

Marshmallow Teddy-Bear
Popcorn Balls

No one knows when the first popcorn ball was formed, but popcorn poppers from ancient times have been found in Peru. You'll need to work quickly to shape these balls, so gather everyone to help.

Makes: **20 popcorn balls (serving size: 1 popcorn ball)**

Know Your Ingredients

Corn is the only cereal grain native to the Americas. Crops were first grown 3,000 to 4,000 years ago by Mesoamericans—people who lived in Central America and Mexico.

Ingredients

50 large marshmallows
1/3 cup butter
20 cups freshly popped popcorn
2 cups teddy-bear-shaped chocolate graham-cracker cookies
    (such as Teddy Grahams)
2-1/2 cups candy corn
Cooking spray

Preparation

1. Combine marshmallows and butter in a Dutch oven or a deep, heavy-bottomed pot. Cook over medium-low heat until melted and smooth, stirring occasionally. Remove from heat.

2. Combine popcorn and cookies in a big bowl.

3. Pour marshmallow mixture over popcorn mixture, tossing to coat. Stir in candy corn.

4. Lightly coat hands with cooking spray. Shape popcorn mixture into 3-inch balls, pressing together firmly. Cool on waxed paper.

5. Wrap balls in plastic wrap. Store in an airtight container for up to 3 days.

Nutritional Information: Calories: 241 | Fat: 4.7 g | Saturated fat: 2.3 g
Monounsaturated fat: 0.9 g | Polyunsaturated fat: 0.3 g | Protein: 2 g | Carbohydrate: 49.3 g
Fiber: 1.5 g | Cholesterol: 8 mg | Iron: 0.6 mg | Sodium: 89 mg | Calcium: 31 mg

Cinnamon-Sugar
Apple Cider Crisp

The apples used in this recipe were named for "Granny" Maria Ann Smith, who first grew the juicy, tart fruit in Australia in 1868.

Makes: **8 servings (serving size: 3/4 cup)**

Know Your Ingredients

Tart and crisp Granny Smith apples are our top choice for this recipe because they hold up best in baking.

Ingredients

1/2 cup all-purpose flour plus 1 tablespoon
1/4 cup granulated sugar plus 2 tablespoons
1/4 cup packed light brown sugar
1/4 cup chilled butter, cut into small pieces
7 cups peeled, cored, sliced Granny Smith apples
   (about 7 medium)
1/3 cup apple cider
1 tablespoon fresh lemon juice
1 teaspoon ground cinnamon
Cooking spray

Preparation

1. Preheat oven to 375°.

2. Combine 1/2 cup flour, 1/4 cup sugar, brown sugar, and butter in a blender or food processor; pulse 4 times or until crumbly. Set aside.

3. Combine apples, cider, 2 tablespoons sugar, lemon juice, 1 tablespoon flour, and cinnamon in a large bowl; toss gently to combine.

4. Coat an 8-inch-square baking dish with cooking spray. Spoon apple mixture into baking dish; sprinkle with crumb mixture.

5. Bake in oven for 40 minutes or until lightly browned. Serve warm.

Feast on This
Try a baked green apple sprinkled with cinnamon and stuffed with raisins.

Nutritional Information: Calories: 224 | Fat: 6 g | Saturated fat: 4 g
Monounsaturated fat: 1.5 g | Polyunsaturated fat: 0.25 g | Protein: 1 g | Carbohydrate: 44 g
Fiber: 5 g | Cholesterol: 15 mg | Iron: 1 mg | Sodium: 43 mg | Calcium: 12 mg

Big 'n' Crunchy
Sugar Cookies

Sparkling sugar cookies are holiday favorites. These goodies, which earn their name from a coating of coarse sugar, have lots of fans.

Makes: 18 cookies (serving size: 1 cookie)

Ingredients

1 cup butter, softened
1 cup granulated sugar
1 large egg
1-1/2 teaspoons vanilla extract
2 cups all-purpose flour
1/2 teaspoon baking powder
1/4 teaspoon salt
Coarse decorating sugars in assorted colors

Preparation

1. Beat butter at medium speed with an electric mixer until creamy. Gradually add sugar, beating until smooth. Add egg and vanilla, beating until blended.

2. In a separate bowl, combine flour, baking powder, and salt. Gradually add to butter mixture, beating just until blended.

3. Shape dough into a ball; cover and chill 2 hours.

4. Preheat oven to 375°. Line baking sheets with parchment paper.

5. Divide dough into 3 portions. Work with 1 portion of dough at a time, storing remaining dough in refrigerator.

6. Shape dough into 1-1/2-inch balls. Roll each ball in decorating sugars.

Sugar Culprits

Here are the food groups that contribute the most added sugar to the American diet:

1. Soft drinks: 33%
2. Candy: 16%
3. Cakes, cookies, and pies: 13%
4. Fruit drinks: 10%
5. Dairy desserts: 9%

Source: American Heart Association

7. Place sugared cookie-dough balls 2 inches apart on baking sheets. Gently press and flatten each ball to 3/4-inch thickness. Repeat steps with next two portions of dough.

8. Bake in oven 13 to 15 minutes or until edges of cookies are lightly browned.

9. Cool 5 minutes on baking sheets, then place cookies directly on wire racks to cool completely.

Nutritional Information: Calories: 189 | Fat: 11 g | Saturated fat: 7 g
Monounsaturated fat: 3 g | Polyunsaturated fat: 0.5 g | Protein: 2 g | Carbohydrate: 22 g
Fiber: 0.5 g | Cholesterol: 39 mg | Iron: 1 mg | Sodium: 82 mg | Calcium: 13 mg

Quick, Heavenly
Berry Trifle

Don't trifle with your loved ones—make them a trifle! This is a light and fresh version of the traditional English dessert. Fresh strawberries and raspberries also work well in this recipe.

Makes: **4 trifles**

Ingredients
Whipped Topping Mixture

1 tablespoon grated lime rind
2 cups reduced-calorie frozen whipped topping, thawed

Berry Mixture

1-1/2 tablespoons fresh lime juice
1 cup blackberries, plus 1/4 cup
1 cup blueberries, plus 1/4 cup

Trifle

2 cups (1/2-inch) cubed angel-food cake

Preparation
Part One: Whipped Topping Mixture

1. Fold lime rind into whipped topping; set aside.

Part Two: Berry Mixture

1. Place lime juice, 1 cup blackberries, and 1 cup blueberries in an 8-inch-square glass dish.

2. Mash berry mixture using the back of a spoon.

Know Your Ingredients

When it's in season, use fresh fruit. When it's not in season, fresh fruit can be tart or flavorless, so go with frozen fruit. Frozen fruit has been picked at the peak of ripeness, so it is often the better choice.

**Feast
on This**
Mashing the berries
releases their juice,
which adds flavor
and moisture to
the cake.

Part Three: Trifle

1. Divide half of the cake cubes evenly among 4 see-through dessert glasses.

2. Spoon half of the berry mixture, then half the whipped topping mixture, into the dessert glasses. Repeat layers with remaining cake cubes, berry mixture, and whipped topping.

3. Top trifles with remaining 1/4 cup blackberries and 1/4 cup blueberries.

Nutritional Information: Calories: 304 | Fat: 20.4 g | Saturated fat: 10 g
Monounsaturated fat: 6 g | Polyunsaturated fat: 4.1 g | Protein: 2.3 g | Carbohydrate: 44.8 g
Fiber: 4 g | Cholesterol: 0 mg | Iron: 0.4 mg | Sodium: 358 mg | Calcium: 40 mg

Glossary

al dente (all-*den*-tay) the texture of cooked pasta when it is soft but still a bit firm inside; in Italian, this phrase means "to the teeth"

all-natural food food without added hormones, antibiotics, sweeteners, food colors, or flavorings

appetizer a small dish of food eaten before a meal

aromatic having a strong, sweet, or spicy smell

bake to cook food by dry heat in an oven

batter a thin mixture of flour, egg, and milk or water; it may include other ingredients

broiler an area of the oven that provides the highest heat and cooks food very quickly

bruschetta (broo-*sket*-ah) grilled bread topped with garlic, olive oil, basil, tomato, onion, and seasonings

calcium an element needed to keep bones strong

calorie the unit of measurement for food energy

canola oil a vegetable oil

carbohydrate the body's main energy source from food

chef a restaurant's top cook, who plans menus and kitchen activities

chickpea a high-protein legume; also called garbanzo bean

chop to cut into small pieces

condensed milk canned milk with some water removed; includes 40% added sugar; it has a caramelized taste and is light brown and very thick

condiment a sauce or seasoning, such as ketchup or mustard, that is added to food to enhance flavor

cornstarch fine, powdery ground corn; it is used to thicken sauces

crustacean (crust-*ay*-shun) an animal with a shell, such as a crab, lobster, or shrimp

cuisine cooking practices and traditions from a specific culture

dextrose a type of sugar found in animals and plants; it is sometimes added to foods

dough a thick mixture of flour, egg, and milk or water; it may include other ingredients

dragnet a net for catching many fish at once by pulling it along the bottom of a body of water

evaporated milk canned milk with 60% of its water removed; it is thick like cream, and has no added sugar

extract liquid taken from a plant; it contains plant's flavor and smell

falafel a deep-fried ball or patty made from ground chickpeas

fiber material in food; it helps regulate the digestive system

fructose a sugar found in naturally sweet foods such as honey and fruit

garbanzo bean *see* chickpea

garnish an ingredient added before serving; it adds to a meal's flavor or appearance

griddle a flat surface for stovetop cooking

hominy corn soaked and ground for easier digestion

hormone a chemical substance made in the body that regulates the activity of certain cells and organs

iron a mineral in the blood that carries oxygen to different parts of the body

jelly-roll pan a baking sheet with sides that are one inch high

julienne to cut food into thin, match-like strips

ladle a long-handled spoon with a deep cup

marinade a sauce used to soak, soften, and flavor meat and fish

marinara sauce a simple tomato sauce with garlic, herbs, and onions

mineral an essential nutrient from water and soil

monounsaturated fat a type of fat found in red meat, whole milk products, nuts, olives, olive oil, and avocados

nutrition the combined elements of food that provide healthy energy to the body

obesity the condition of being very overweight

orzo (*ore*-zoh) pasta shaped like small rice grains

phytochemical a natural element essential to plants

polyunsaturated fat a type of fat in nuts, seeds, fish, and leafy greens

preheat to heat the oven, pan, or pot before cooking begins

processed food food changed from its natural state, often with human-made ingredients added to allow the food to last longer on the shelf or to improve flavor

producer a person, company, or country that grows and supplies food

protein an essential element that helps human tissue grow and heal; it can be obtained from meat, fish, eggs, legumes, and milk products

puree (pure-*ay*) to blend cooked food until it's creamy, as in a dip or a soup

rind the outer layer of certain fruits, vegetables, and cheeses

roast to cook uncovered by a dry heat source such as an oven

rotisserie a small broiler with a motor-driven stick that turns meat over a flame

saturated fat a type of fat in meat, butter, cheese, milk, palm oil, and coconut oil

sauté (saw-*tay*) to cook food in a pan with a small amount of oil, butter, or other fat

savory having a pleasant flavor or smell without sweetness

skewer a thin metal or wooden stick used to hold pieces of food together

sodium a salt in foods or beverages, often added as a seasoning or preservative

springform pan a round cake pan with a removable bottom

sucrose sugar

sweeteners natural and artificially produced sugar substitutes; not all are good for the body, even when they have fewer calories than sugar

utensil an instrument used in a kitchen, such as a knife, fork, or spoon

vitamin an essential nutrient made by animals and plants

wok a metal pan with a curved bottom; it is used to cook Chinese cuisine

zest the skin of a citrus fruit that is used as flavoring

155

Recipe Index

Breakfasts

Apricot-Almond Bits 'n' Pieces Granola............18

Bacon and Egg Breakfast Pizzas 24

Banana-Chocolate Fab French Toast 32

Blueberry and Maple-Pecan
    Granola Parfaits.......................................17

Chocolate Chip WOW! Waffles 30

Cinnamon Streusel Applesauce Muffins 22

Classic Banana Bread...................................36

Fun and Fruity De-lish Oatmeal......................38

Ham and Swiss Breakfast Grillers 28

Lemon Tart Poppy Seed Muffins 20

Maple-Pecan Granola Crunch.........................16

Mixed Fruit Sunshine Smoothie.......................34

Sausage and Egg Dusty-Trail Burritos.............26

Lunches

Barbecue Chicken Picnic Sandwich..................60

Cheese Lover's Grilled Cheese 56

Cheesy Roll-Up Pigs in Blankets 62

Creamy Tomato Alphabet Soup 66

Egg Salad Sandwich Stacks 48

Life of the Party Pizza Sticks..........................58

Mangia! Margherita Panini............................68

Mouthwatering Monte Cristo Sandwich...........70

Peanut Butter & Jelly Bagel Grillers.................44

Pesto Presto! Pasta Salad..............................46

Smooth and Savory Cheese Spread.................50

Soba Noodles with Sweet & Spicy Shrimp........52

Soup-er Quick Chicken Noodle Soup 64

Tropical Breeze Chicken Salad 54

Wrapped-Tight Turkey Bites...........................42

Sides and Snacks

Brown and Green Buttered Beans 90

Cheesy Chive Potato Chips.............................89

Coconut + Fruit + Sushi Rice = Frushi 82

Creamy Ranch Dip..75

Incredible Edible Nutty Putty 78

Make Mine Marshmallow Nice Crispy Bars.....79

Oatmeal-Raisin Energizer Bars 80

On the Go Munchies Mix................................77

Protein-Packed Peanut Dip.............................76

Roasted Sweet-Potato Fries 88

Summertime Broccoli Slaw Salad 84

Tangy, Cheesy Broccoli Trees 91

Tasty Lemon-Sage Spaghetti Squash 92

Toasted Mozzarella Cheese Poppers 86

Yummm-kin Pumpkin Dip...............................74

Dinners

Chicken Drumette Dipping Wings 116

Corn and Bacon Chowder Crocks 110

Crushed and Crusty Chips-and-Fish 98

Fast and Delicious Sloppy-Joe Sliders............ 126

Grilled Chicken Super Kebabs 114

Guacamole Fish Tacos 112

Have It Your Way Veggie Burgers 120

Home-Baked Chicken Fingers 108

Nature's Nectar Glazed Salmon 128

On Top of Old Smoky Spaghetti
   with Meatballs 124

Pineapple-Bacon Globe-Trotter Pizzas 96

Shrimp "Fried" Confetti Rice 122

Special Pork Posole Soup 118

Spicy-Sweet Quesadilla Treats 106

Three-Bean Chunky Chili 102

'Wave It Up Meat-Loaf Mugs 104

Wheel in the Sky Tortilla Pie 100

Desserts

1, 2, 3–Freeze! Chocolate Ice Cream............. 138

All-Time Favorite Choc Chip Cookies............. 142

Big 'n' Crunchy Sugar Cookies...................... 150

Cinnamon-Sugar Apple Cider Crisp.............. 148

Creamy Berry Fruit Pops 140

Easy & Perfect Vanilla Pudding 136

Gingersnap Chilly Willies............................ 132

Here Comes Simon the Centipede!............... 144

Marshmallow Teddy-Bear Popcorn Balls 146

Melt in Your Mouth Chocolate Cupcakes...... 134

Quick, Heavenly Berry Trifle 152

 Index

Banana-Exporting Countries 37

Cereals with the Most Sugar 19

Cheese Producers...................................... 57

Chocolate-Loving Countries 31

Cinnamon Growers 23

Grape-Growing Countries 43

Nutrients in Oatmeal.................................. 39

Olive-Oil Producers.................................... 69

Poppy-Seed-Producing Countries 20

Sugar Culprits... 151

U.S. Crops 111

Index

Canada 111

India... 65, 100

Italy 47, 59

Japan 53, 99

Philippines 100

General Index

A

apple(s)
    cinnamon-sugar apple cider crisp, 148
    Granny Smith, 148
    origins of applesauce, 23
apricots
    dried, in granola, 18
    in history, 35
    in smoothies, 34
avocados, 112

B

bagel
    first bagel in history, 45
banana(s)
    bread, 36
    top 5 banana-exporting countries, 37
    types of, 36
bars
    marshmallow crispy, 79
    oatmeal-raisin, 80
beans
    garbanzo, 120
    kidney, 102
    pinto, 102
blueberries
    in parfaits, 17
    in trifles, 152
    selecting, 17
brain freeze, 139
bread crumbs, 87
broccoli
    as part of the cruciferous family of vegetables, 91
    production in the U.S., 85
    slaw, 84
    trees, 91
burgers
    veggie, 120
    sloppy-joe sliders, 126
buttermilk, 75

C

Canadian bacon, 97
canned pineapple, 97
Carver, George Washington, 78
cheese
    grilled cheese sandwiches, 56
    how to store, 56
    in quesadillas, 106
    mozzarella, 86
    Parmesan, 109
    poppers, 86
    spread, 50
    Swiss, 29
    top 5 producers, 57
chicken
    adobo, 100
    drumettes, 116
    fingers, 108
    in town names, 64
    kebabs, 114
    noodle soup, 64
    rotisserie, 54
    salad, 54
    tandoori, 100
Children's Day, 53
chili, 102
chocolate
    benefitial nutrients in, 143
    buttercream frosting, 135
    chip cookies, 142
    cupcakes, 134
    ice cream, 138
    top 5 chocolate-loving countries, 31
    world's largest chocolate bar, 142
cinnamon
    in apple crisp, 148
    in streusel topping for muffins, 22
    top 5 growers, 23
coconut
    milk in frushi, 82
    saturated fat in, 82
cookies
    chocolate chip, 142
    gingersnap, 132
    Oreo, 144
    sugar, 150

cumin, 60
cupcakes
    chocolate, 134
    different flavors, 135

D

dancer's diet, 81
dip
    creamy ranch, 75
    peanut, 76
    pumpkin, 74

E

eggs
    how to separate egg whites, 30
    in history, 25
    salad sandwiches, 48

F

fish
    and-chips, 98
    glazed salmon, 128
    tacos, 112
    yellowfish tuna, 113
French toast, 32
fruit
    freezing, 152
    pops, 140

G

garlic
    in ancient Egypt, 93
    phytochemicals in, 93
ginger
    chewing to relieve upset stomach, 123
    gingersnap cookies, 132
    as a disease-fighter, 117
    root, 132
granola
    invention of, 16
green beans
    buttered, 90
    consumption on Thanksgiving Day, 90

green onions
 how to curl, 116

L

lemon
 in poppy seed muffins, 20
 rind, 21
Likness, Lizzie Marie, 22

M

marshmallow
 crispy bars, 79
 popcorn balls, 146
meatballs, 124
microwave(s)
 description of, 104
 how to microwave bacon, 24
muffins
 cinnamon streusel applesauce, 22
 English, 29
 lemon tart poppy seed, 22

N

National Pigs-in-a-Blanket Day, 62
National Popcorn Month, 147
National Potato Chip Day, 98
nuts
 hazelnuts, 32
 in granola, 16, 18
 pecans, 38

O

oatmeal
 top 5 nutrients in, 39

P

panko, 87
pasta
 average consumption per person
  in North America, 125
 salad with pesto sauce, 46
 spaghetti with meatballs, 124
 soba noodles with shrimp, 52

peanut butter
 and jelly bagel grillers, 44
peanut(s)
 different names for, 78
 dip, 76
 protein in, 76
pesto sauce, 47
pimiento, 50
pizza
 bacon an egg breakfast, 24
 pineapple-bacon, 96
 sticks, 58
popcorn
 balls, 146
 National Popcorn Month, 147
potato
 chips, 89
 chips-and-fish, 98
 National Potato Chip Day, 98

R

ranch salad dressing, 42
rice
 and chicken salad, 54
 protein in fried, 122
 shrimp "fried," 122

S

salad
 broccoli slaw, 84
 chicken and rice, 54
 egg-salad sandwiches, 48
 pasta salad with pesto sauce, 46
salmon
 anadromous, 128
 glazed, 128
 wild and farm-raised, 129
sandwich
 barbecue chicken, 60
 grilled cheese, 56
 ham and cheese grillers, 28
 Margherita panini, 68
 Monte Cristo, 70
 peanut butter and jelly bagel, 44

shrimp
 soba noodles with, 52
soup
 chicken noodle, 64
 corn and bacon chowder, 110
 posole, 118
 shark-fin, banned, 66
 tomato alphabet, 66
squash, 92
Stillwater Harvest Fest and Giant
  Pumpkin Weigh-Off, 74
sugar
 added to food, 141
 brown, 80
 cookies, 150
 culprits, 151
 top 5 cereals with the most, 19
sushi, 82
sweet potato wedges, baked, 48, 88

T

tomato
 in paninis, 68
 soup, 66
tortilla(s)
 corn and flour, 107
 in history, 27
 pie, 100
turkey wraps, 42

V

vanilla
 beans, 137
 leading growers of, 136
 pudding, 136
vegetarian(s)
 burgers, 120
 famous, 121

W

waffles, 30
White House's Chefs Move to
  Schools program, 71

How Sweet It Is!

There are 32 words hidden in this word search. They may go forward, backward, up, down, or diagonally. And they may overlap. Circle the words from the list below. (We've done one for you.) Then write the leftover letters in order from top to bottom, left to right. They will spell out a very sweet sentence.

~~APPLES~~	MITT
BAKE	MIX
BUTTER	NUTS
CHEFS	OVEN
CINNAMON	PASTRY
DOUGH	POT
EGGS	SAGE
FAT	SPOON
FLOUR	STIR
FOOD	SWEET
FORK	SWIRL
FROSTING	TARTS
HOT	TEETH
LIST	TIN
MILK	VANILLA
MINT	WHISK

```
M  I  T  T     B  A  K  E     E     H     O     T
K     I     C     I  N     N     A     M  O     N        F
D     O     U     G     H     D     V     I     S        O
O     W     H     I     S     K     A     N     L     L        R
O     T     A     R     T     S     N        T     O     I        K
F     C     H     E     F     S        S     I     S        I        R
E     R     S     W     I     R     L     L     O     L     I        T
B        C     O     P     A     H     L     O     N     C        O
L     U     A     S     O     P     A     S     T     R     Y
N     U     T     S     T     O     P     O     V     E     G     N
T     E     E     T     H     I     N     L     T     G     I     M
A     S     W     E     E     T     N     E     E        G     I  X
F        F     L     O     U     R     E     G     A     S
```

___ ___ ___ ___ ___ ___

___ ___ ___ ___ ___ ___ ___

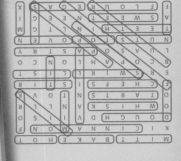